The Blue Collar Follies

By Daren Peel

JOHN DECKER

THANKS FOR YOUR SERVICE

Sand River Publishing
Holly, Michigan

© 2022 Daren Peel All Rights Reserved
No part of this book may be reproduced or transmitted in any form
or by any means, electronic or mechanical, including photocopying,
recording, or any information storage and retrieval system,
without written permission from Sand River Publishing.

Printed in the United States of America
Sand River Publishing
Second Edition

Dedication

To my family and friends, and all the
blue collar people everywhere, this is for you.

I want to thank Tex Ragsdale and B.K. Taylor for
helping me make this dream come true.

Tex Ragsdale is a longtime writer for advertising, the internet, commercial fiction, and independent feature films, as well as for Hollywood studios Universal, Disney, and Nickelodeon.

B. Taylor is a nationally known illustrator and writer who has contributed to ch varied media as Jim Henson's Muppets, National Lampoon, Walt Disney feature animation, Scholastic publishing, Nickelodeon, and ABC's Home Improvement.

About the Author

I'm Daren Peel. I was born in Memphis, Tennessee, but grew up in Ontario, Canada, and so I naturally hunted, fished, camped and followed hockey. And still do today.

I'm a Union Master Plumber and an independent handyman, doing both jobs for the past 35 years. Before that I worked in lumber mills, made car batteries, picked mushrooms, cut firewood, worked as a security guard, and was a trapper, just to name a few.

I consider myself a blue collar guy, born and bred. It's who I am. And to me, "blue collar" is a badge of honor.

Over the years I've collected funny, sometimes crazy stories from working men and women in all kinds of trades and occupations, people who I've known and worked with. My friends kept asking me what I was going to do with all the stories … so I decided to write a book!

Because I love to give back by doing volunteer work and donating to small local charities, a percentage of book sales will go to good causes around the country.

Just a Touch

Here's an embarrassing story that happened to a handyman friend of mine named Bert. He can laugh about it now, but he said at the time that it made him feel like he was in an old Three Stooges movie, playing the really dumb role of Curly.

He was working for a very finicky and eccentric older woman in a luxury, two-story condo. She originally contracted for him to do some plumbing. But she knew that he also did a lot of handyman-type jobs.

After the relatively minor plumbing job was done, she soon had him doing all kinds of stuff like hanging doors, changing light fixtures, installing ceiling fans, you name it. He didn't think he was ever going to get out of there.

But Bert drew the line at painting and wallpapering. He hated to do both of those jobs. So he called in a couple of friends who specialized in them. And what the customer wanted there wasn't easy, either. For instance, the kitchen had to be papered in black and white stripes, floor to ceiling, and of course the stripes had to line up perfectly. Fortunately Bert didn't have to do it!

But it was finally finished. He and his little crew were getting ready to leave. All that needed to be done was to settle up the bill, which had grown pretty substantial.

Before the lady of the house signed the check, though, she had just one more little job for Bert.

He knew he should've seen that coming. Anyway Bert agreed to do it.

Now this was at the end of the day. He and his friends were tired and wanted to get home. Since they all came in his truck, they would have to wait while he did what she asked.

Sounded pretty simple.

One of the upper rooms in her condo was not being cooled very well by the central air conditioning. So she had bought a window unit that she wanted Bert to install. Just open the window, set it in the frame, and plug it in.

How hard could it be?

He walked up the stairs to the room where he had to install the air conditioner. Everything was very quiet, since everyone was outside waiting for him.

Over in the corner of the room was the air conditioning unit. Didn't look like too big a deal. So Bert opened the window, which faced the front of the house and the street where his friends and their employer stood waiting. He waved. They motioned for him to hurry it up.

So he turned back into the room to get the air conditioner. Wasn't too heavy, but it was awkward. He carried it over and set it on the sill of the open window, getting ready to shift it into place.

About to make the final adjustment to the AC unit, Bert just touched it. He swears – he just *touched* it!

Since it was just balanced in the open window, that was all it took.

Yep. Just what you're thinking. It toppled right out the second-floor window.

Bert tried to grab the cord as it went by ... but it was no use. It was jerked through his hand.

"Look out below!" he yelled.

There was a tremendous *CRASH!* Which sounded like more than just the unit hitting the ground.

It was.

The window air conditioner fell *right on top* of the big central condenser unit! Both were smashed into a pile of junk. Expensive junk.

Bert remembers that he turned back into the room and slumped down on the floor, thinking about the check *he* would have to write to *her!*

A Leg Up

An electrician friend of mine named Marty moved to New York City a few years ago to do custom work for a lot of the rich and famous folks on Park Avenue. He got the reputation of being able to do any kind of job, no matter how unusual or difficult.

And many of these people *were* difficult to work for. They wanted things done *their* way – and were used to getting it.

That was the downside. The upside was that they were willing to pay for what they wanted. And pay very well. But you had to deliver, with no screw-ups. Marty was a guy who could always deliver.

What made his job a little tougher was that most of these high-end customers lived in the very old, classic New York townhouses or apartment buildings. The rooms were often small and narrow, sometimes going up three or even four stories. That meant that Marty usually had less space to work in than he would have liked.

But he could always find a way. Like they say, that's why he got the big bucks.

Anyway, one day he got a call from the personal assistant of a famous concert pianist. (These types of customers didn't make the calls themselves, of course. They had "people" to do it for them.)

The great man wanted an electrical outlet installed in his "piano room." He liked to practice in the middle of the night, with his favorite antique lamp on the piano to see the sheet music, and he absolutely did *not* want an extension cord running across his beautiful hardwood floors.

Okay, Marty told the woman who called – no problem.

So he went over to the pianist's home. Sure enough, it was one of those narrow townhouses jammed beside a row of others overlooking Central Park. Cost a few million, easy, thought Marty.

A young woman named Jennifer, the pianist's assistant, showed him in and took him up to the piano room. Marty didn't really know what to expect. It was a narrow, rather small room ... with a huge grand piano just about filling it. Jennifer proceeded to tell Marty what the customer wanted.

"He would like the plug on the wall next to the piano," she said. "Oh, and if you could get that done before he gets home, that would be great."

Marty looked at his watch. Time would be tight. "I'll have to drill up from the room below, once I see where all the wiring is."

"Whatever," she said. "It's just storage down there."

So Marty decided where to put the plug in the wall next to the piano and carefully cut a hole for the plug's electrical box.

He measured everything, and went down to the storage room underneath. He measured again, calculating where his drill bit would come up inside the wall.

Marty cut a small panel out of the ceiling, found the wiring and got out an extended drill bit. He figured he'd come up inside the wall, right next to the piano.

But when he started to drill, the bit went up ... and up ... and up. Still sending down wood shavings.

What the heck? He should be inside the empty space in the wall.

He pulled the bit out and checked it. It had gone up three feet – still in solid wood!

Something was not right.

He ran up the stairs, looking around for Jennifer, hoping she wasn't around. The coast was clear.

In the piano room, he went to the hole he had cut in the wall. He was able to reach his hand inside and feel for a hole in the floor.

Nothing.

He looked all around. No hole in the hardwood floor anywhere. At least *that* was a good sign. What was he drilling into?

But then he had a horrible thought.

Marty went to the piano ... and shoved it slightly to one side. Sure enough – there was a hole in the floor, lined up perfectly *under the piano leg*. His measurement had been slightly off.

And he had hollowed out the piano leg!

Too Tight for Comfort

Everybody knows that occasionally tools and materials "disappear" from workplaces across the country. Usually it's nothing much – like an extra wrench or screwdriver that manages to find its way into a personal tool bag.

Now I'm not condoning stealing from the company, but it does happen. And it doesn't get to be a big deal until someone gets so greedy that they can't help but get caught. Like a friend of mine whom I'll call Frank.

Frank was a welder at a trucking company, and he also did welding on the side for friends and paying customers. Nights and weekends, Frank was kept pretty busy.

So that meant he needed a lot of materials ... which he didn't always buy. He regularly helped himself to the company supply of welding rods, gloves, masks, and even an occasional acetylene tank! Nobody ever said anything, so Frank got more and more bold about taking things home.

But one day he went too far.

It was the end of his shift, and Frank was walking through the plant toward the gate and the guardhouse just inside it. The night was cold, and Frank was wearing a bulky jacket. He was huffing and puffing and seemed to have a hard time walking.

"Hey, Frank!" one of his buddies called out. "You okay?"

"Yeah," gasped Frank. "Just tired."

Frank continued on, heading for the gate. Then he began to stagger.

Another buddy caught up to him. "You need some help, Frank? You don't look so good."

"I'm fine!" Frank said angrily, and shoved the guy away. "Let me get to my truck. I'll be okay!"

But he didn't look okay as he continued on, stumbling and wheezing as if he couldn't catch his breath.

Finally, just outside the guardhouse, Frank collapsed on the ground, flopping around like a beached seal. The guards came rushing out.

Frank couldn't talk, but he was gasping and pointing to his chest and making frantic motions.

"He's having a heart attack!" yelled one of the guards.

"I know CPR!" said the other. "Help me get his jacket open!"

When Frank heard that, he tried to fight them off. No way did he want them to open his jacket. But then he passed out, stone cold.

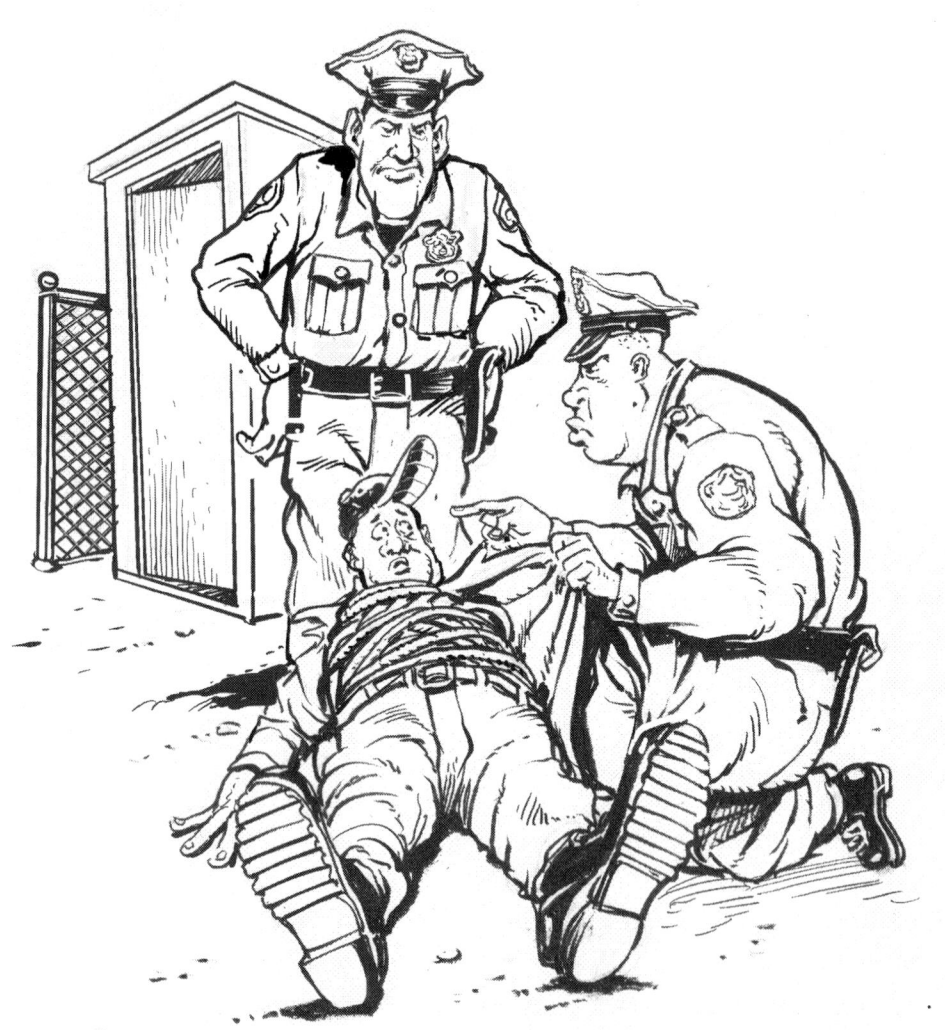

The guards hurriedly got the zipper undone, opened the jacket … and stepped back in surprise. No wonder Frank couldn't breathe – and it wasn't a heart attack, either.

Frank was trying to make off with *welding cables.* He had wrapped them around his chest, under his jacket. But as he walked, the heavy cables sunk down, winding tighter and tighter around his chest, like a steel boa constrictor!

Once the guards got the cables off him, Frank was okay. A free man – free of his job, that is!

Getting a Lift

Marge was the top fork-lift operator at a downtown construction site where a high-rise was going up. She had a lot of experience and could make her lift truck really maneuver.

Believe me, this was a valuable talent where work space was tight. And nowhere is it as tight as in a high-rise, sandwiched between other buildings. A lot of her work involved riding the freight elevator in her lift truck, carrying steel and other materials to the various floors under construction.

She got along great with everybody, but one particular foreman, Chuck, had it in for her for some reason or another. He would try to assign her the toughest, dirtiest jobs, usually involving picking up the dumpsters with her fork-lift and emptying them.

But he also enjoyed making her pick up the portable outhouses on the various floors and bring them down the elevator for flushing out. In the hot summer, this wasn't a nice job.

"Hey, Marge!" Chuck yelled one day, "make sure you get the porta-johns on the upper floors before three o'clock!"

"I'm workin' on it!" she yelled back, secretly fuming.

And instead of going to get the porta-johns, she continued lifting the steel beams and construction materials. She'd get around to the johns when she was good and ready!

A couple of hours later, Chuck yelled at her again. "Pick up those johns yet?"

"Next trip," she called back, going up in the elevator. She could see that he was getting really ticked off. He knew she was avoiding the nasty job.

"Make sure you do!" he yelled. "Or you're on report!"

Grumbling, Marge figured she'd better pick up the porta-johns right away. So Marge rode the elevator in her lift truck to the top floor and started working her way down. It was a long, slow, *stinking* business.

The more she thought about Chuck being on her case all day, the madder she got. If only there was some way to pay him back without getting into trouble …

16

Marge reached the last floor with the final porta-john and expertly slipped her forks under it. She was so good that it didn't jiggle a bit as she picked it up and started toward the elevator.

Suddenly she heard thumps and bumps coming from somewhere – but where? She looked around, saw nothing, and rolled right into the elevator.

Then she heard a muffled scream, more thumps – and then the door of the porta-john burst open! Chuck the foreman came flying out, his pants down around his ankles!

All the guys standing around killed themselves laughing.

"Well, Chuck," Marge called out with a satisfied grin, "you *told* me to pick 'em up!"

Here, Kitty, Kitty...

John Murphy, who everyone called "Murph," was an expert drywaller. In fact, he was an *artist* with drywall. He'd been doing it for thirty years, and there wasn't any problem he couldn't handle when it came to drywall.

He was so good that he told me he couldn't remember the last time he had to tear out and fix any part of a drywall job. Murph did the job once – and it was right. He prided himself on that.

But sometimes a job came along where you didn't have complete control. Or a problem cropped up that you just couldn't foresee. Well, Mrs. Fenster's living room was one of those.

She was a fussy little old lady who liked cats, had a lot of money, and a lot of time on her hands. She didn't like the living room because it had a strange little alcove that had always bothered her.

Now, no one else would worry about such a thing. But, like I said, Mrs. Fenster didn't have much else to do. So she got Murph's name from a friend and called him.

"I'd like you to cover that awful alcove up!" she told him. "It's really too small for anything. Can you do that?"

"No problem," said Murph confidently, as he made the list of the materials he'd need. This would be a sweet job, he thought. Piece of cake. He'd be able to just sail through it.

"Will there be a lot of dust?" she asked.

"Some," said Murph. "I have to sand the mud after it dries."

Mrs. Fenster looked alarmed. "*Mud?* On my walls?"

"That's just a name for the plaster that covers the seams," Murph said with a chuckle.

"Oh. Well, I don't want anything to hurt my kitties. They think of this room as theirs, you know."

Murph looked at the three cats lying around on the furniture. "They'll hardly know I'm here," he said.

So Murph started to work the next day. Sure enough, the cats did think they owned the place. They never left the room no matter how much noise he made with his screw-gun.

Every once in awhile, Mrs. Fenster would poke her head in and call, "Be careful of my kitties, now!"

Murphy got tired of hearing that, and was glad to finally be done with the first coat of mud. And the wall was one of his typically smooth jobs.

When he called Mrs. Fenster in to see it, she was properly impressed. "Oh my," she said to Murph, "it's beautiful!" Then she turned to the cats. "Isn't it, dears?"

The two cats in the room looked up from their chairs. Uh oh. *Two* cats. Mrs. Fenster gasped. "Where's Annabelle?"

Then, from behind Murph's perfect job came a faint *mee-oww...*

That's a Mouthful!

One winter night I got a call from a lady who said she had a *big* plumbing problem. I really hate those late-night calls, especially when it's about five below outside. But she was desperate.

When I got there, the lady of the house came to the door in just a bathrobe, soaking wet. She may have had a big problem ... but she was also a big lady. Maybe three hundred pounds or so.

She led me upstairs to her bathroom, and there was an old-fashioned tub, the kind with feet. It was still filled with dirty, soapy bathwater.

"The water won't go down!" she wailed. "And it's starting to leak all over the floor!"

Sure enough, the drain was blocked up.

"Don't worry," I tried to reassure her. "I'll take a look."

Since the bathroom was on the second floor, the only access to the drain was through the wall of a porch on the first floor. An *unheated* porch. I had to get up on a ladder near the porch ceiling, bust through the wall – and hope my fingers didn't freeze off!

Well, I worked on those pipes for a couple of hours. I cut and soldered and jacked them around. Still couldn't clear the blockage.

The P-trap was full of water and starting to freeze. I had to do something.

Every once in awhile the very large lady would poke her head out the door and shriek: "Please hurry! I'm gonna have a flood!"

I figured I had to get the standing water out of the trap to see what was going on. What to do?

There was one option that would probably work. I didn't really want to do it, but I had no choice.

So I went back to the truck and got a length of plastic tubing and a bucket.

Climbing the ladder again, I stuck one end of the tubing into the trap ... and the other end into my mouth. I had to create a siphon to get the water out.

This'll be quick, I told myself. Go for it!

Very carefully I sucked on the tube – and the blockage broke loose in the pipe. There was a rush of water down the tube and *into my mouth*!

My cheeks filled up with flux, bits of solder, the lady's dirty bathwater ... and whatever other little goodies might've been in there!

I couldn't spit it out fast enough!

My teeth went all bitter, like I'd eaten a green banana. They felt dry, coated with awful gunk. I almost lost my supper right then and there!

As the rest of the bathwater poured out of the pipe, I stumbled down from the ladder, choking and coughing.

The lady came out on the porch grinning with relief. "You're a genius!" she said. "The tub is empty."

"Yeah," I croaked. "I just swallowed most of it!"

"You poor man," she said sympathetically. "Then I guess you don't want something to drink ...."

Butt of the Joke

We all know there's a certain amount of horseplay that goes on in every job. And some more than others, usually depending on how dangerous the job is. Practical jokes and kidding around are often good stress relievers. But sometimes they can get pretty risky.

I met a couple of roofers, Pat and Freddy, who were not ones to take chances and endanger everybody ... but they also had their share of laughs. Especially when a new guy came on the job. They felt he had to be broken in.

Morris was young and cocky. He made himself pretty obnoxious from the first day, boasting about how no job was too tough for him. Naturally Pat and Freddy started planning how to "get" him.

They were all working on a new subdivision – huge, expensive houses with equally huge roofs. All the while they laid shingles, Morris would go on and on about the tough jobs he'd had in the past.

"This job is nothing," he'd say. "You guys are a buncha wimps! I've worked on roofs so steep ... man, you can't imagine!"

"Never even been a little nervous?" Freddy asked, egging him on.

"Nah! Not me, pal!"

"You're saying nothing scares you, eh?" asked Pat.

"No way," said Morris. "Anytime you show fear up here – you're done! There's just no room for it."

"Is that so?" said Pat.

"Damn straight," Morris said smugly.

Pat and Freddy looked at each other and smiled.

They had to be careful that the foreman wasn't watching. And they also didn't want to do anything that might result in Morris getting hurt. They just wanted to shake him up a little, so he wouldn't be such a bigmouth.

Pat and Freddy waited until the three of them were working on a section of roof that wasn't very steep. They were cutting vent holes in the plywood with a Skilsaw, then installing vents.

As usual, Morris was going on and on about how tough he was and how he'd seen it all.

"Yeah, I remember this church roof I was working on, laying real slate, and ..." Blah, blah, blah.

22

Pat flashed Freddy the signal. This was it. They couldn't take any more. Now was the time.

They waited until Morris had his back turned to them. He was bending over, installing a vent ... and continuing to talk. They both snuck up quietly in back of him.

Suddenly Pat started up the Skilsaw!

At the same time, Freddy reached out and scratched Morris' butt with a roofing nail!

Morris let out a *screech* and leaped into the air, coming down on all fours, hugging the roof. The other two just about died laughing.

And that was the end of Morris' boasting.

Hangin' Around

Ted and Mario were two "tin-bangers" who were installing sheet metal ductwork high in a wall, near the ceiling of a factory.

They were using what is sometimes called a "boom lift." It's also sometimes called a "man lift." You've seen them – a long, hydraulic arm with a bucket at the end to stand in, that has control levers for raising or lowering it. There was also a set of controls in the truck that carried the lift and arm.

Well, Ted and Mario raised themselves way up to the opening for the ductwork. They attached their safety harnesses to a ceiling beam, and started to shove the sheet metal into the hole. But the bucket couldn't quite raise them high enough.

So Ted climbed up on the edge of the bucket – not a good idea. But he figured it was only for a couple of minutes, just to get the last of the ductwork in.

Then his foot hit the hydraulic control for lowering the bucket – and it suddenly dropped about ten feet.

Mario was jerked right out of the bucket by his harness! He and Ted were left dangling from the ceiling beam by their harnesses and shouting for somebody down below to *raise the damn bucket!*

Call a Taxi ... dermist

A friend of mine owns a small taxidermist shop up in Canada, north of Toronto, right in the middle of hunting country. He gets a lot of business mounting trophies and making fur rugs.

In fact, everybody in the area comes to Jake not only because he does great work, but also because his shop is a kind of central meeting place for hunters. Everybody stops in there sooner or later.

So one day a guy he knew came running into the shop all excited.

"I did it, Jake, I finally did it!" he yelled.

"Calm down, Harry," Jake said. "What did you do?"

"Got me a *wolf!* Right here in town! Can you believe it?"

"A wolf?"

"Sure as all get-out!" Harry said. "It was prowling around the house. I just ran out with the twelve-gauge and slug load. Nailed him right by the back porch!"

"Well, let's see him."

Harry brought in the carcass and set it down in front of Jake.

"What do you think?" he asked proudly.

"Beautiful pelt," Jake said. "What do you want me to do with it?"

"A rug!" Harry said. A wolfskin rug! Always wanted one."

"Can do," said Jake. "I'm not real busy now. Come back at the end of the week."

"Okay, see you then," said Harry happily as he went out, thinking about his wolfskin rug.

But Jake did get busy suddenly. He had several rush jobs come up ... and he forgot about Harry's rug. Until a few days before Harry was due to pick it up.

So Jake rushed the job through – and he had it done in a couple of days. He draped the new rug over the counter so Harry could get a good look at it when he came in to pick it up.

Then Jake went into the back room to catch up on some paperwork. He heard the door open – and was startled by a blood-curdling yell.

Jake rushed out front to the counter, and there was Charlie Robinson, who lived a few streets away, staring with horror at the rug.

"Charlie, what's wrong?" Jake said.

"That ... that *rug!*" Charlie could barely choke the words out.

"What about it? I made it from the wolf Harry McCoy shot."

"Wolf?! That's no damn wolf!" Charlie shouted. That's Rebel, my prize husky dog! He's been missing for a week!"

He grabbed up the rug and rushed out.

"Hey!" Jake yelled. "Where you going?"

"To find McCoy. I'm gonna make a rug outta *him!*"

A Moon Out Tonight

A trucker I know named Paul had a girlfriend who worked in a beauty salon. The hairdressers' chairs were lined up in a row so that they all had a view of the street through the wide window. His girlfriend Charlene's chair was right in the middle of the row.

Whenever Paul was making a run in his truck, he'd make sure he drove by the beauty salon to wave at Charlene. Sometimes Paul would even blow kisses as he zoomed by. Pretty soon the other people in the shop started to kid her about it.

"That boyfriend of yours sure doesn't mind making a fool out of himself in public," said one hairdresser, laughing.

"Well, *I* happen to think it's very romantic," said another.

Charlene smiled. "Paul likes to show his feelings," she said.

Charlene and Paul went on like that for months. On Valentine's Day Paul would drive by holding a big heart-shaped balloon out the truck window that said I LOVE YOU. On Charlene's birthday, he drove by waving a flashing sign that said HAPPY BIRTHDAY.

"Paul likes to show his feelings," Charlene would always say, pleased at all the attention.

But then a few days went by ... and no Paul.

The other hairdressers noticed that Charlene was looking glum. Her friend Gina went over to her chair. "What's wrong? Where's Paul?" she asked her.

"Oh, we've been fighting," Charlene said. "He's mad at me."

"Anything serious?" Gina asked.

"He thinks I'm seeing another guy," Charlene said. "But I'm not! I don't know where he got that crazy idea."

"Well, he'll get over it," Gina said. "We all miss him 'showing his feelings.'"

Just then one of the other hairdressers pointed out the window and called out. "Hey – here he comes!"

Sure enough, Paul was walking down the street toward the beauty shop with an angry look on his face. Then he stopped, right in front of the big window, with everybody staring out at him.

He glared at Charlene through the window – then suddenly turned around and dropped his pants! Paul *mooned* the entire beauty salon!

But at the same moment, his wallet popped out of his pants and dropped to the ground, just as he ran off.

"Well, *that's* showing his feelings!" said Charlene. And everybody began to laugh.

But it wasn't so funny to Paul. The police picked up his wallet and were waiting for him when he got home – to charge him with indecent exposure.

And showing more than his feelings.

All Wound Up

This little episode actually happened to me at the beginning of my plumbing apprenticeship. The last thing I ever wanted to do was tell the foreman I couldn't do something.

So when we had to drill through a concrete wall one day, and the foreman brought out a brand-new hammer drill – naturally I volunteered to handle it. Even though I had never run one before.

The drill was at the end of a long extension cord. And as I turned it on and it started to bite into the concrete, I suddenly realized something was wrong. Since I'm left-handed, the full-power switch was under my palm – and it locked open!

The drill bit snagged a steel reinforcing rod in the concrete and stuck! But the drill itself didn't stop running. It jerked out of my hands and spun around and around – and jammed in the wall. It wound up the extension cord like a giant ball of yarn ... until it yanked the other end out of the outlet and finally stopped. Close call!

The Hot Seat

McCorkle was one of those old-time guys who wouldn't change his ways no matter what. He had worked on an assembly line in a Detroit auto plant all his life and had his routine down pat.

On his breaks he would always head for the john, whether he had to actually go or not. He'd bring the newspaper, sit down on the closed toilet lid and read, or take a nap. Sometimes you'd walk by and see his feet under the stall ... then see the newspaper drop to the floor. He'd fallen asleep sitting up!

Well, one thing you were not supposed to do anymore is smoke in the john. The new rules forbid it. But of course McCorkle didn't pay any attention. He'd always smoked in the john – and was going to keep on doing it.

Until one day when there was a muffled *explosion* from the men's room – and McCorkle came running out, batting at the seat of his pants! He'd been sitting on the lid, having a smoke, and tossed the butt into the toilet under him. *BOOM!*

What he didn't know was that the water had drained out of the trap – and the burning butt hit a pocket of methane sewer gas!

That gave *him* a burning butt! And it was the last time McCorkle ever smoked in the john.

Tripped Up

Two cop friends of mine told me this story about a little bet they once had. Marvin and Art were partners and were an unusual-looking pair together. Marvin was slight and skinny, while Art was pretty hefty. In fact, they reminded everyone of Laurel and Hardy.

It was a continuing argument that Art had to lose some weight. Marvin was always bugging him about it – for his own good.

"Y'know ..." Marvin said, "there's a department policy about being overweight. The sergeant's gonna get after you."

"Yeah, yeah," Art said, getting annoyed. "I'm workin' on it."

"I saw you workin' on it at the doughnut shop the other day," Marvin said.

"Hey, I'm not too fat to perform my duty," said Art. "I can do anything you can!"

"What about chasing a suspect?" Marvin asked. "You couldn't run somebody down."

"Care to bet on that?" asked Art. "Loser buys doughnuts."

"You're on," said Marvin.

"Okay, I'll take the chase next time we get one," said Art. "We'll see who's out of shape and who isn't."

The opportunity to settle the bet soon presented itself. A few nights later, Marvin and Art got a call to respond to a breaking and entering in the warehouse district of their city.

They pulled up in their squad car at the building where the break-in was reported. Sure enough, as they shined their flashlights around, they spotted a recently broken window, right next to the door. Somebody had just gone in – or out.

"Looks like I'll have to go through the window," Marvin said, grinning at Art. "You sure can't make it."

Art was about to come back at him, when suddenly they heard a noise behind them. They turned and saw a figure running away into the dark alley between the buildings.

"He's already out!" yelled Marvin.

"I'm on him!" shouted Art – and took off running. But he wasn't able to keep it up for long. The suspect was getting away.

Worse than that, he would have to admit to Marvin that he couldn't cut it. He'd lose their bet and have to put up with endless digs about his weight.

But then in the darkness ahead, he heard a crash ... and shined his light forward.

There was the suspect, tangled in a pile of trash cans. Across the alley stretched a *chain* about knee-high with a rusty "NO TRESPASSING" sign hanging from it. The suspect had tripped over the chain – and took a dive into the trash cans!

Art quickly cuffed him and hauled him back to the squad car, where an amazed Marvin was waiting.

Later that night, Marvin bought doughnuts – and never said another word about Art's weight.

And Art never said a word about the chain.

Hair Today

A carpenter from Quebec sent me this story. It made him a little embarrassed, so I won't use his real name. Let's call him Pierre.

Pierre's union was having an upcoming Christmas party. It was always a really big deal, with lots of people.

Then Pierre found out that one of his old friends was retiring. He was asked to give a little speech at the Christmas party about the years they had worked together.

He had no problem speaking in public. In fact, he liked to get up in front of a group and tell stories. He was actually looking forward to it.

Now, Pierre always had a thing about his hair. He was very proud of it, spent a lot of time combing it just right.

Only trouble was, it was getting pretty gray.

All it took was for a couple of the guys he worked with to make some comments: "Hey, Pierre! You a grandfather yet?" Or: "When are you retiring, Pierre?"

He laughed along with them, but it was starting to get him down.

Pierre asked his wife if she thought he looked old.

"No ... not really," she said hesitantly.

"What do you mean 'not really'?" he asked. He knew by her tone of voice that she wasn't telling the whole truth.

"It's just your hair," she admitted. "It's pretty gray."

"Well, what can I do?" Pierre asked, starting to panic. "I don't want to look like an old man at the Christmas party! I have to get up in front of everybody!"

"You could dye your hair," she said.

Pierre was horrified. Real men didn't dye their hair! "Forget it!" he said. "I wouldn't think of doing that!"

But as the Christmas party approached, he did think about it. In fact, he bought a bottle of hair dye. *Black* hair dye.

The night before the party, Pierre went out into the garage without telling his wife and opened the dye package. He looked at the instructions and realized that he had forgotten one small thing:

He couldn't read English very well. And there were no instructions in French.

"Oh well," he said to himself. "How hard can it be?"

So he poured the dye on his head. He didn't know how long to leave it on, so he decided to give it a good shot. After all, he wanted to really cover the gray, didn't he? He decided to take a little nap ... and woke up three hours later!

When he went into the house, his wife shrieked: "Pierre! What have you done to yourself?"

He rushed to a mirror and saw what had happened. The dye had not only blackened his hair – but had also stained his face! And no matter how much he washed, it wouldn't come off.

So Pierre went to the Christmas party, gave his speech, and picked up a new nickname:

Raccoon.

The Big Squeeze

Big Max was a millwright in a large paper manufacturing plant. Naturally he was called Big Max because he was fairly small. In fact he was one of the smallest guys I ever knew who could still do heavy physical labor with the best of them. Nothing slowed him down.

And many times, his short stature actually helped. The foreman would often call on him to crawl into a tight space and work where nobody else could.

One of the places in the paper plant where his particular talent was valuable was in the big vessels or holding tanks. Max had to squeeze through a kind of porthole opening and work inside all day then maneuver his way out at the end of the day.

Usually this was a piece of cake for Big Max. But one cool morning in the summer, Max crawled into the vessel and started to work. No problem so far.

But as the day went on, the heat started to rise. Max noticed that sweat was pouring down his face.

"Hey, out there!" he called to the foreman through the porthole. "It's hotter than hell in here! What's the temperature?"

"I read 110!" the foreman called back. "Can you stick it out to finish the job?"

"I'll make it," said Max. "But then I'm outta here fast!"

And Max did finish. He tossed his tools out through the porthole and started to crawl out feet first as always.

But something was wrong. Now he didn't fit.

What was going on? he wondered. He could always do it before. Maybe it was his coveralls; they were damp and soaked with sweat. He threw them off and stripped down to his underwear and tried again to slip out the porthole feet first ...

And got stuck at the waist. His upper body was still in the vessel, with his butt and legs outside.

"HAAAALP!" he yelled, his voice muffled by the giant vessel.

Pretty soon a small crowd began to gather just outside, laughing at Max's predicament.

"Bet I know what the problem is," Rick the foreman yelled to Max. "You're all swollen up from the heat!"

"Well, do something!" Max yelled back. "Get me out!"

"Hang in there, Max! I got an idea!" Rick said, and called for a couple of the guys to bring over a hose used for rinsing down the tanks.

"What are you gonna do?" Max called nervously.

"Got to cool you down!" Rick yelled – and turned on the hose.

"That's CO-O-O-OLD!" Max shrieked as the water hit him.

"That's the whole idea!" Rick yelled back, laughing.

And sure enough – it worked. Max slid out of the porthole wet and chilly, but all in one piece.

"Hey, Big Max," one of the guys said. "Glad to have you back. But I think you're shrunk even more than usual!"

Max couldn't help but laugh right along with them.

Something Between Us

A bricklayer in California named Craig sent me this story about the time he and his wife Julie had to move quickly so he could take a new job.

It was one of those moves where they had no time to pack carefully. Mostly they ended up tossing everything into boxes and jamming them into a U-Haul truck. We've all done that.

But the truck they had rented was just a little too small for all their boxes, and there was no time to rent a different one. Craig and Julie had to cram every available square inch full in the truck itself ... and then stack boxes between them in the front seat as well. The truck cab was so full they couldn't even see each other!

Now, Craig was very excited about the job and the possibilities for the future. And he was one of those people who loved to "think out loud." Julie could hardly get a word in edgewise. He chattered as he drove.

"Man, that new subdivision where I'll be working is so huge, it might be good for years of work!" he said.

"Uh huh," Julie answered from behind the pile of boxes.

"And the area is just exploding," he continued. "I tell you, Julie, we're making the right move!"

"Mm hmm," she said, as Craig went on and on.

After hours on the road, they stopped for gas and something to eat. In the diner, Craig couldn't contain himself. He was so full of new plans. All Julie could do was listen.

As they walked back to the truck, Craig kept talking and Julie followed. He climbed up behind the wheel, revved up the engine and took off.

It was about a half hour down the road, when Craig finally had enough of hearing the sound of his own voice.

"Well, I'll shut up now, Julie," he said. "You tell me what you think of all this."

No answer.

"Julie?"

Still no answer.

Craig tried to see over the pile of boxes that separated them, but he couldn't. She's probably asleep, he thought. But ... something nagged at him.

Finally he pulled the truck over, got out, and walked over to the passenger side ...

No Julie!

He'd been talking so much, he'd driven off before she could get into the truck!

She might not have had a lot to say on the first leg of the trip – but she sure gave him an earful after he went back and picked her up.

Hot Lick

This one happened to me one day when I was fixing the drain on a lady's kitchen sink.

I was in a tight spot, wedged into the sink cabinet, trying to get enough leverage on my wrench to loosen the P-trap. The lower cabinet doors were all open so I could get as much light and air as I could in there.

But that wasn't all I got.

The lady's huge Doberman suddenly stuck his head in through one of the open doors and looked at me, inches away from my face, while I was struggling under the sink. Now, this is one mean-looking dog. I have to say that he made me nervous – but what could I do? I couldn't move.

Then I heard the lady's voice in the kitchen, "Oh, don't worry about Peaches," she called out to me. "He's a real sweetheart. So gentle, wouldn't harm a fly!"

At this point, staring me right in the eye, Peaches made a little growling sound. Somehow he didn't seem like much of a sweetheart to me.

But then Peaches pulled his head out of the cabinet and disappeared. I breathed a sigh of relief and went on working.

A few minutes later, I turned my head – and there was Peaches, eye-to-eye with me again!

I was so startled that I dropped my wrench. Peaches moved closer to my face. I was still so wedged in that I couldn't move.

This is it, I thought to myself, he's gonna bite my face off!

But instead, Peaches stuck his big, wet tongue out and *licked* my face all over.

I was so relieved that I laughed. "Take it easy, boy," I told him. "I'd rather wash up *after* the job is done!"

But Peaches wouldn't leave me alone. I was still under the sink, wrestling with the pipes – and Peaches was constantly licking my face! And the lady of the house had gone out to the store, so she couldn't do anything to stop him.

I had to do something or I couldn't finish the job. But what? I pulled myself out from under the sink, stood up and stretched ... and spotted one of those tiny bottles of Cajun hot sauce in the cupboard.

An idea popped into my head.

I poured a few drops into my hand and rubbed it onto my face. The stuff made my eyes water, but I went back to work. And waited.

Soon, there was Peaches again, his head stuck under the sink, licking my face.

But not for long.

Peaches let out a doggie-screech and disappeared! I heard his claws scurrying across the kitchen floor. Then I heard water slurping. Lots of water.

Now, since the water was turned off in the house while I was working, I figured there was only one place he could be drinking from.

Just at that moment, I heard the front door slam and the lady's voice yelling: "Peaches! Stop drinking out of the toilet!"

One Big Dump

Maybe you know that a guy's truck often becomes part of his personality. He identifies with it. If anything bad happens to the truck or somebody messes with it, it's like they were messing with the person himself. Dean was a guy just like that.

He had a Ford 150 that had been through hell and back with him, and he was really proud of that truck. Dean had done a lot of work on the engine and body over the years and had it just the way he wanted it. If somebody had offered him a new 150 in an even trade, he would've turned them down.

He hauled everything from firewood to cinder blocks to 60-pound bags of cement – you name it. Dean knew that truck was built to take the heavy loads. And he was confident to the point of bragging about it.

"I'm tellin' you guys," he'd say over and over to his friends, "nothing stops this baby!"

"Yeah, yeah," they would say, having heard it all before.

But then one day, Dean's truck was put to the test. Or rather, Dean's high opinion of it was.

He had to go pick up a load of gravel and deliver it to a job site where they were pouring cement. And the work was behind schedule.

The foreman pulled him aside before he left.

"I don't want you making a lot of trips all the way out to the gravel pit," the foreman said.

"I hear you," Dean said, nodding.

"Get as much as you can in one load, okay?"

"No problem," said Dean. "You got the right guy – and the right truck!"

And off he went.

When Dean got to the gravel pit, he pulled his truck up under the loader and motioned for the operator to start pouring the gravel into the bed.

Now, the usual procedure is to sort of dribble in the load so that a truck takes it on gradually, rather than in one big dump. And that's what the operator started to do.

But Dean kept looking at his watch. "C'mon, c'mon!" he yelled, "I haven't got all day!"

The operator increased the stream of gravel pouring into the truck bed, but Dean was getting more and more impatient as he watched it slowly fill.

"Let's go! I got a job to do! Pour it on – gimme the *whole load!*"

The operator yelled back, "You don't want it all at once! Your truck –"

"My truck can take anything! JUST DO IT!"

Well, by that time, the operator had had enough. He yanked on the lever ... and the entire load of gravel poured into Dean's truck.

All four tires blew at once! The frame crashed down onto the ground, and gravel spilled everywhere!

And nobody heard Dean bragging about his truck ... while he unloaded it *by hand*, so they could fix the tires!

Who's Who?

A journeyman electrician told me this one — and begged me not to use his real name, because he got into a bit of trouble over it. So let's just call him Dan.

Dan had been around awhile and really knew his job. Nobody could tell him what to do, and he resented anyone trying to. That's mostly because he *did* know more than anybody else.

But it's the nature of bosses to think that they know more. It's sort of like in their job description.

Well, one day Dan was training a new apprentice. He was good at this because no question could stump him. He always had a quick response ... sometimes *too* quick.

Dan was holding the ladder while the apprentice Barbara (one of the first women electricians in this particular shop) was up at the top of the ladder working on the cable trays.

Every once and a while, Barb would call down a question and Dan would answer. He was sipping a cup of coffee and generally taking it easy.

Eric, one of the higher-ups, walked by on a kind of inspection tour, just sort of sniffing around. He couldn't help but notice Dan lounging against the ladder.

"Working hard?" Eric asked sarcastically as he walked by.

"Always," said Dan. He gave Eric a big grin.

Of course, Eric never noticed Barb up on the ladder. He thought Dan was just goofing off.

Barb called down: "Who was that?"

"Aw, just Eric, trying to make himself feel important," Dan called back up.

About a half hour later, Dan was still holding the ladder for Barb. Now he was munching contentedly on a doughnut.

Eric came by again. He looked Dan up and down.

"What's going on here?" he said.

"I'm eating a doughnut," said Dan. Nothing and no one ever shook him up.

"You haven't moved from the last time I was here!" said Eric, getting himself cranked up.

"I'm workin'," said Dan quietly. Dan got quiet when he was starting to get mad.

"I came by here the first time, and you're drinking coffee! Next time you're eating a doughnut!" yelled Eric.

Barb looked down from up on top of the ladder. Uh oh, she thought. She knew what was coming, and it wasn't good.

"What's it to *you*, pal?" asked Dan through gritted teeth. "I do my job. Why don't you go do yours?"

"You ... you can't talk to me that way!" sputtered Eric. *"Do you know who I am?"*

"Hey, Barb!" Dan yelled up. "Go call the paramedics! This guy doesn't know who the heck he is!"

Decoy This!

This story is about pure frustration. A friend of mine, Doug, is a maintenance man for a large, high-tech company in Michigan. They had just built a new, state-of-the-art headquarters building. You know the kind – all glass and stainless steel, on precisely cut grass, surrounded by a crystal-clear retention pond.

All this was mostly to impress customers. The big boss didn't want anything less than perfection for their corporate image. But he didn't figure on the geese.

Every fall, Canada geese migrate south over Michigan ... but a lot of them stop off and never leave. And this company's reflecting pond was like a magnet for them. They plopped down in the water and decided to stay.

What's more, once the employees started to feed them, they *really* didn't want to leave. Pretty soon they started to mess the place up as only big birds can do. The perfect lawn and the perfect glass building were soon covered with ... crap.

The big boss called Doug and his maintenance crew in. "Get rid of those damn birds!" he told them. "I don't care how you do it!"

Doug and his men tried chasing them off. They came right back. The men got air horns ... and the geese honked back at them. Nothing worked.

"I got an idea," Doug told his guys. "We'll decoy them away, over on the other side of the road!"

"With what?" asked Mitch, not one of his brightest workers.

"With *decoys*, of course! What else?" said Doug.

So they got a lot of expensive rubber decoys and set them out on a swampy pond across the road. Doug grouped the decoys, hoping to make it look very inviting.

Then they chased the geese off the good pond and went home for the night. The next morning, the geese were back.

"Guess the decoys didn't work," said Doug.

"Nope," said Mitch. "Because somebody *stole* them. They're gone!"

"Then there's only one thing to do now," said Doug. "We'll fix it so the dang geese can't get to the pond at all!"

So he and his guys began stringing heavy-gauge wire around the pond, goose-high. The thinking was that the geese could maybe fly over it, but they couldn't easily get in and out to get food. They might get frustrated and leave.

At first it seemed to be working. The geese didn't get the idea that they could fly over the wire. They just milled around outside it in confusion.

But then the company directed everybody to park in a different parking lot due to construction. People had to walk by the pond on a path they weren't accustomed to.

And the next morning, as Doug was getting out of his truck, he saw a guy with a briefcase running from the parking lot, late.

"Watch out for the –" he started to yell.

But the latecomer tripped over the wire and took a dive into the pond!

"– goose-wire!" Doug finished.

The entire web of wire collapsed in a tangle ... and the geese quickly joined the latecomer in the pond. After that, nobody bothered them again.

A Strange Flush

If you believe amazing coincidences can actually happen – and I do – then maybe you'll believe this story. When I heard it from a policeman friend of mine, I found it hard to believe at first. But he swears it's true.

Derek was a cop in Chicago for a long time, and he was doing pretty well in terms of pay. In fact, he put a lot of his money into real estate investments. He would buy houses, fix them up, and then rent them out.

Pretty soon he was spending as much time looking after his houses as he was being a cop. And they took a lot of looking after. Anyone who deals with renters can tell you that.

The family in this one house in particular was always causing him problems. Things would get broken in the house, and they would call Derek to get them fixed – even though it was most likely the renters' fault.

The first few times he took care of the problem, like repairing the window that mysteriously broke or the hole in the roof that appeared all by itself – right under their son's tree house!

So when Gary, the guy who was renting the house with his wife and son, called Derek and told him the toilet was plugged, Derek was about fed up.

"What did you try to flush down it?" he asked.

"Just the usual!" said Gary. "Whatever *anybody* flushes down a toilet. Do I have to spell it out for you?"

"I get the picture," said Derek.

"You gotta get over here quick! It's an emergency!" Gary almost yelled.

"Take it easy," said Derek. "I'm just getting off my patrol now. I'll come right over and take a look."

So Derek didn't stop to get his truck and tools, he drove to the house in his squad car, still in his uniform.

Inside, Gary, and his wife and son, were anxiously looking at the water spilling over the top of the toilet bowl. Derek stopped at the entrance to the bathroom.

"Let's get one thing straight," he said to Gary. "If I find something down there that you put in, *you're* paying for the clean-up and damage."

"Okay, okay," Gary quickly agreed.

"Get me a wire coat hanger," Derek said, since he didn't have his tools with him.

Gary's wife brought one. Derek rolled up his uniform sleeve and straightened the hanger out with a small hook on the end. He pushed it down the toilet ... and felt it snag something. Something hard and metallic.

He pulled and struggled. Finally, whatever it was slid around the bend in the toilet. He hauled it up, caught on the hook end of the wire. Both parents turned to their son with looks that could kill.

So what did Officer Derek pull out of the toilet?

A toy police car!

Big Mouth

The guy who told me this story got a lot of satisfaction out of telling it. It made him laugh, but it also gave him the feeling that justice had been done.

You know how it is. Somebody speeds past you in a car, almost sideswiping you. You wish that *just once* there was a cop around to see it – and then farther down the road you see the speed demon pulled over. *Yes!* Justice!

Anyway, this story happened at a place where the "tin bangers" worked. That is, where they made sheet metal products like furnace ductwork.

The guys who worked there had been bothered for a long time by Tony, one of the mechanics who loved to talk. About anything at all. Not only did Tony talk a lot, but he was also an expert on everything, or thought he was.

Any subject you could bring up, Tony knew more about it than you did. Or at least, he said he did. And he would *not* shut up, morning to night. Guys started requesting the night shift just to get away from him.

One of the guys, Al, started talking about restoring a classic Mustang. He liked working on the Mustang because parts were relatively easy to get and cheap.

"Ha!" chimed in Tony. "That's nothin'! I once restored a '58 Nash Metropolitan! Try finding parts for that baby! Most of 'em had to be machined – and that wasn't cheap, let me tell you."

"Well, I sold the Mustang for three times what I paid for it," said Al.

Tony, smiled his big toothy grin. "I sold the Metropolitan for *five times* what I paid!" he said. "It was a gem!"

And blah, blah, blah. On and on. Pretty soon the guys ran for cover, as usual.

Now here's where the justice part comes in. Remember I said that Tony had a big toothy grin? He did – but those teeth were false! And *bad* false. Must've bought them at a thrift shop or something.

So Tony was up on the shop roof one day, working on repairing a hole. There were several guys down on the shop floor right under him, getting ready to hoist some roofing material up to him.

While Tony worked, he kept talking. Not about the job at hand, but about whatever popped into his head. Only now, he was pretty high up, so he had to *shout* down to the guys below.

Not only did they have to listen to his yakking, but it was *loud* yakking! This was just too much.

But then fate took a hand.

Suddenly, in the middle of his high-volume blabbing, his false teeth *popped right out of his mouth!* They fell through the hole in the roof ... and shattered on the concrete floor below like a handful of Chicklets!

Just as the guys below stopped laughing, the lunch whistle blew.

"Hey, Tony," one of them yelled up. "Guess it's *soup* for you today!"

"Yeah," another one added, "Through a straw!"

"Ahhh," said a third. "A meal in peace and quiet."

What's Up ... Dock?

Mike is a small-engine mechanic in the suburbs around Chicago, where a lot of the very wealthy people have built huge homes on Lake Michigan. He gets a lot of work from them, just keeping their lawn tractors, snow blowers, and power boats going.

Now, you have to realize, that these people are "old money." They buy something expensive and keep it for many years, usually still in the family.

And many of these people, even though they live in huge old mansions, are often pretty cheap. They've got the money, but they hate to spend it, especially on repairs around the house. Sometimes those mansions can look good from a distance, but are actually pretty run-down when you get close up.

That was the case with Mrs. Hamilton's house. She was a rich old lady who would call Mike to fix the machines and appliances around her place, but wouldn't do much to fix the house itself. If fact, it was falling down around the edges.

But she took particular pride in her boat. It was one of those inboard Chris-Craft jobs from the 40's. You know the type I'm talking about. All polished wood and brass, with leather seats in the tiny cockpit and a huge engine under the deck. It was almost too beautiful to put in the water.

Mrs. Hamilton kept it in a boathouse on the shore that was like the rest of her mansion – kind of tumbledown. And the dock was just as bad. It looked like it was ready to collapse into the lake.

So when she called Mike to work on the boat's engine because it wasn't running right, he felt a little shaky walking out on the dock.

"Is this thing safe?" he asked her.

"Oh, don't worry," Mrs. Hamilton said, following close behind him. "This old dock has been standing for seventy-five years, and will be here another seventy-five!"

They got the boat out of the boathouse and tied it up at the dock so Mike could climb inside and work on it. As she always did, Mrs. Hamilton stood right nearby, making comments, asking questions, and generally driving him crazy while he worked.

"I think it's the carburetor. Do you think it's the carburetor? Maybe it's the spark plugs. How many spark plugs are there? What's that thing sticking out over there ... ?" And on and on.

Mike tried his best to ignore her, but it wasn't easy.

He just kept working away on the boat's engine while Mrs. Hamilton paced back and forth on the dock. She was getting a little impatient because it was taking so long.

"Aren't you done yet?" she said. "It's getting awfully late. I think you should test the engine right now!"

He really wasn't ready, but Mike had learned not to argue with her. Hurrying, he climbed into the cockpit and started the boat's engine – and took off from the dock. From behind him, Mike heard a cracking sound, a scream, and a huge splash.

He suddenly realized: she rushed him so much that *he had forgotten to untie the boat from the dock!*

When he looked back, there was Mrs. Hamilton sitting in the lake, and she didn't look happy. The boat had jerked the old dock right out from under her!

Boxed In

Calvin and Wally worked for a heating and cooling company some years ago that specialized in furnaces. The large metal cabinets of the past have shrunk quite a bit in recent times, but back then they were bulky and heavy as all get-out!

Well, Cal and Wally had to deliver a furnace and install it by the end of the day. That was a condition that the homeowner laid down at the time of purchase. When their boss asked them if they could do it, Wally was confident.

"No problem," he said.

"There better not be," said the boss, "or this guy's going to be really ticked off – and he'll cancel the sale."

So Cal and Wally trucked the furnace over to the house where they were supposed to install it. Nobody was home when they got there, but their boss had given Wally a key so they could let themselves in.

Right off the bat, things didn't go well. The furnace was to be installed in the basement, and they had to bring it down a very narrow flight of stairs then turn a tight corner.

"Better measure it before we start," Wally said.

Cal got out of his tape and did. It was going to be close. "Should just make it," Cal said.

"Okay, I'll go first," said Wally.

Since they decided that there was no room for their dolly, they started to carry it down the stairs one step at a time. Wally on the bottom would lift it down, with Cal holding it from above to keep it from tipping forward. It was a very stressful process.

Near the bottom of the steps, Wally called a halt. "Hold it right there," he gasped. "I gotta rest a minute."

But as Cal tried to hold the big cabinet, he felt his fingers slipping. "Uh oh," he said. "I'm losin' it!"

And the whole unit tipped forward.

It bumped down the last couple of steps and pinned Wally against the bottom wall. It wasn't actually crushing him, just boxing him in so tight he couldn't move. And neither one of them had any leverage to move the unit.

"You okay?" Cal called nervously. He couldn't see Wally behind the big furnace.

"Yeah, I'm all right. Better get the dolly outta the truck!" Wally yelled. "Maybe we can move it with that!"

"Don't go anywhere!" Cal called as he bounded up the stairs.

"Where am I gonna *go?*" Wally muttered.

Cal ran to the truck, pulled out the dolly, and was already figuring out how they could move the furnace. It could work! They could still meet the deadline for installing the unit.

But then he tried to open the door to the basement that he had closed behind him when he ran out. It was locked.

And Wally had the key.

Out of the Pipe

Ralph is a plumber in Louisville, and he sent me this story. He had picked up a contract in his spare time doing repairs on a run-down apartment building. It was in a very old – and tough – part of the city. Ralph wasn't too thrilled about taking the project on, but the pay was very good.

His first job was to replace a lot of the toilet bowls in the building. As you might expect, it was a pretty dirty operation. Ralph was already beginning to doubt the wisdom of signing the contract.

He had to carry the new bowls up several flights of stairs, pull the old wall-mounted ones off, and install the new ones. With the ancient, rusty plumbing, it wasn't easy.

Ralph was struggling with the last toilet of the day, wondering how he ever got himself into this, when he finally got the old toilet off and the new one lined up with the wall pipe. He was pushing it forward, when …

Suddenly a large, fat *rat* popped out of the pipe! It hopped onto the toilet lid right in front of Ralph's face … and snarled at him!

Ralph dropped the toilet – smashing it – and got the hell outta there! He was *done* with that job, contract or no contract!

Home Cooking

Did you ever think about buying a rental property for some quick and easy income? Just sit back and collect the cash, right? Well, it's not that easy.

I've taken care of rental properties myself, and have heard pretty wild stories from other guys who do the same. Here's one of them.

A friend of mine, Gordon, owned a house in a nice residential area of a Chicago suburb. He had rented it out for a number of years and had to do quite a bit of work on it, just to keep it in shape.

Many renters don't take care of places they don't own. They let the house run down, and sometimes just plain wreck the joint. And often they try to put one over on the landlord about one thing or another.

Gordon felt that this particular house was jinxed. Every single tenant he'd ever had in it had given him some kind of grief.

So when Gordon went to rent this house again after the last tenants had cleared out – and after repairing the damage their kids had done – he vowed he would cover all the bases this time.

Two very nice older women were going to rent the place. They seemed perfectly trustworthy. But still Gordon laid down the law: "No pets, no kids, no waterbeds, no vehicles parked in the living room or any other room, no rollerblades on the floors, no indoor archery practice, no ..."

And on and on. He tried to think of everything, so he could avoid every bad experience he'd had over the years.

The women smiled sweetly and agreed to all his conditions. So he rented the house to them.

They seemed to be model tenants. The place looked great when Gordon would drive by. The yard was always nice and neat, everything shipshape.

When he would stop in, just to see how things were going and maybe make a few little repairs, the two tenants welcomed him warmly. They had decorated the inside like a cozy old farmhouse.

"It always smells so good in here," he said to one of the women. "Like fresh baked bread or something."

"Oh, yes," she smiled. "We like to do a little baking."

So Gordon went on his way and finally relaxed. It appeared that he had found the perfect renters. Maybe the house wasn't jinxed anymore!

Months went by, and Gordon hadn't stopped in at the house for some time. The rent was always on time, and nothing needed to be fixed. Things were going so well. But one day he just decided to check anyway.

He knocked at the door, and when there was no answer, he let himself in with his key.

The wonderful fresh bread smell hit him again as he stepped in.

But when he took another step – *his foot crashed right through the floor!* Then he heard shrieks of surprise from the basement.

Gordon pulled himself out and went down to see what the hell was going on. He found that the two women had set up a whole bakery right in the basement! The moisture from the several ovens going all the time had rotted out the flooring.

"Didn't I tell you all the rules before I rented to you?" asked Gordon angrily.

"But you never said we couldn't have a *bakery*," one of the women replied innocently.

No-Luck Truck

There's a buddy of mine who's in the landscaping business. Todd has been at it for quite a while and has built up a good list of customers over the years.

He used to pretty much do it all himself – cut lawns, trim trees and bushes, design and install landscaping – whatever needed to be done. In those early days of his business, he only had to worry about himself and maybe one other guy. So he had a very efficient operation.

But as Todd's business grew, he had to hire more and more people, buy and maintain more equipment, and run several more trucks. Todd hardly did any of the actual work any more. He spent most of his day just keeping track of his workers and the status of the jobs.

Equipment repair was an especially big headache. It seemed like at least once a day Todd would get an emergency call that some crucial piece of equipment was out of commission. But a lot of the problem had to do with the low quality of the help.

Like Todd once got a call from one of his guys about the bagging mower. "It's broke," the guy said.

"What's wrong with it?" Todd asked.

"Won't pick up leaves."

Todd found that you had to ask a lot of specific questions to get any information at all, and that was all he could get. When he drove over to the job and examined the bagging mower, he found that the guy hadn't lifted the mulch gate! No wonder it wasn't picking up leaves – they couldn't get into the bag! And the guy had been cutting that way for a week!

Typical. Like the call from another of his men, Norm, that one of his trucks had a smashed tailgate. It was all crunched in, Norm told him. They couldn't get the mowers out.

Todd knew he had to start the line of questions.

"What happened to the tail gate?" he asked.

"Don't know," said Norm. "Wasn't my fault."

Over the years, Todd had found that these were two all-purpose answers when something went wrong. (1) I don't know, and (2) it wasn't my fault.

"I think somebody hit the back of the truck," Norm added helpfully.

Todd perked up. A rear-end collision! That meant he could probably collect some decent insurance money and fix up the truck. It was his oldest one.

"Did you get the driver's name and number?" Todd asked anxiously.

"Uh, yeah. It's Miller."

Todd thought that sounded familiar. "Miller ... ?"

"*Dave* Miller," Norm said. "You know – the guy who drives your other truck."

Let Us Spray

Recently I heard from a friend of mine who's a commercial air-conditioning/refrigeration mechanic. He spends a lot of time up on top of buildings working on those huge cooling units.

Bernie told me about the time he and his partner Joe were called downtown to one of those giant supermarkets. The air-conditioning had gone out. And that day it was about 105 degrees.

The manager was waiting for them.

"You boys have gotta fix this fast," he told them impatiently. "Can't afford to have you wasting any time. Better get at it!"

"No problem," said Bernie.

The trouble was, the unit wasn't on the roof, but in the space between the ceiling and the roof. Bernie and Joe climbed up there and were immediately hit by an awful smell!

Looking around, they realized that the employees must've thrown the remains of their lunches up into the space from below, just to get rid of the scraps!

The floor was littered with half-eaten sandwiches, food wrappers, bottles and cans, all kinds of junk. To reach the big air-conditioning unit, they had to pick their way through the trash.

"Man, does this stink!" said Bernie, as he pulled along a work light on the end of a long extension cord.

"Hotter than hell, too," said Joe.

"Like workin' in a garbage dump," agreed Bernie.

They reached the air-conditioning unit, got out their tools and started to work. But whenever they needed to reach another part of the unit, they had to shovel the garbage away, just to get at it.

"Bring the light over here," said Joe.

Bernie started to pull the cord over, and somewhere way back behind them, the plug came out. Now they were in the dark, except for a tiny bit of light coming in from a crack on the roof.

"Great," said Bernie. "What else could go wrong?"

He was about to find out.

Suddenly Joe tripped over some debris – and kicked a full can of beer!

The can flew through the air ... and hit a threaded rod sticking up from the air-conditioning unit. The rod speared it – and beer sprayed everywhere!

Bernie and Joe stumbled around in the heat and darkness, getting covered in garbage and beer. Cursing and sputtering, they made their way back to the ceiling access hatch and climbed back down.

They were a mess.

The supermarket manager was waiting for them with a disapproving frown.

"You guys smell like a brewery!" he said. "And look at all that food! What in the world were you doing up there, having lunch?"

A Close Shave

This story comes from up in Minnesota, where a guy I know runs a mink farm. That's right, a place where they raise those animals they make expensive fur coats out of.

Now, a lot of people are against that, but as for myself, I don't see the difference between raising cattle for beef and leather. Besides that, I've been a hunter all my life. I've seen minks in the wild, and they're certainly not cute, lovable little critters. They're more like weasels. *Nasty* weasels, at that.

Anyway, at this mink farm, Chris the owner gives tours to people who are interested in the whole process. They want to see where their coat comes from.

But as you might imagine, most people don't have a *clue* as to how an animal like a mink turns into a beautiful, luxurious coat.

Chris' favorite story involves one of these tourists, an older woman who dressed like she thought she was in Florida rather than northern Minnesota. Stretch pants and lots of gold jewelry.

Chris was giving his standard talk on the number of minks in a coat. I don't remember what the actual figure was, but it was a lot. This lady peered through her cats-eye glasses at all the minks running around in the pens and turned to Chris.

"My goodness!" she said. "I had no idea it took so many to make a coat!"

"Oh, yes ma'am," Chris said.

"I don't see why," she said. "I mean, since you can re-use them, and all."

Chris was baffled. "I'm sorry. I don't understand. *Re-use* them?"

"Of course, young man," she said, in a tone of voice that showed she thought Chris was an idiot. "Just tell me, how many times can you take their fur off?"

"Take their fur off? You mean, skin them?"

"Yes, whatever. How many times?"

Then it dawned on Chris. She thought you *sheared* minks like sheep, and then the fur grew back and you could do it again! He couldn't believe it! But then he decided to have a little fun with her.

"You can only do it twice, ma'am," he told her with a straight face. "After that, they tend to get a little uncooperative."

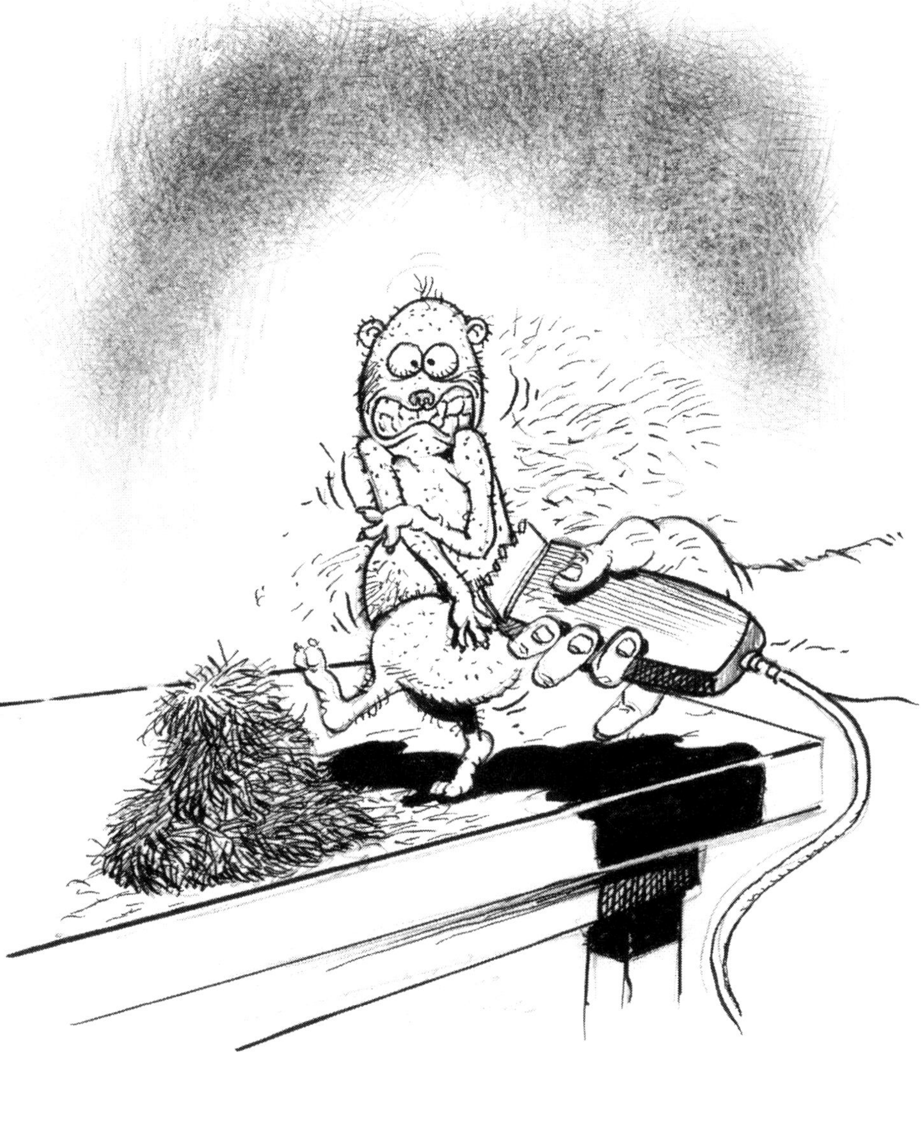

Up on the Roof

Were you ever completely baffled in a work situation? I mean, no matter what you did, you couldn't figure out what could be wrong?

Well, a plumber friend of mine, Bob, and his helper Ray, were called to a woman's home to fix a blocked drain. Seemed like a run-of-the-mill job, at first. The water wouldn't go down in the sink in the second floor bathroom.

"Let's check the P-trap," said Bob.

Ray began taking it off from under the sink. "All clear," said Ray, peering into the trap.

They looked at the hole in the bathroom wall where they had removed the drainpipe. Black gunk was oozing out of it.

"Better get the snake," said Bob.

All they had in the truck was a small ten-footer, but they figured that was all they needed. The blockage had to be somewhere between the sink and the toilet, a distance of only five feet or so behind the wall.

Ray started cranking the snake in by hand. "That's as far as she'll go," he said finally. "Has to be clear now."

They pulled the snake out, wiped off the black gunk, and put the P-trap back together. The sink was still blocked.

"What in the world is going on?" said Bob, scratching his head.

"Might have to bust out the wall," said Ray.

There was a gasp from behind them. The lady of the house had overheard. "Oh no, please don't!" she said. "I just got all this new tile!"

"Don't worry, Ma'am," Bob said, trying to reassure her. "There's something else we can try."

"What is it?" she asked.

"We need power. And a longer snake. I don't know where that blockage is, but we'll reach it with that, for sure."

"Please hurry," she pleaded. "The roofers are coming any time now, and I'd like to get done with this first."

So Bob and Ray went down to the rental shop and got a thirty-five foot, power-driven snake.

When they arrived back at the house, they saw that the roofing crew was already there, preparing to tear all the old shingles off.

They knew that the homeowner wouldn't be happy, but there was nothing else they could do. They brought the power snake up into the bathroom and started to feed it into the wall pipe.

It made a terrific racket as it chewed its way along inside the pipe. It just kept going ... and going ... and going. Until all thirty-five feet were in – and still hadn't hit any blockage.

Suddenly they heard shouting outside. And loud *thumps* on the roof just above them. Pieces of something went dropping by the bathroom window.

They looked out and saw the roofers on the lawn outside, motioning them to come out. The roofers were killing themselves laughing.

When Bob and Ray came out of the house and looked back up where the roofers were pointing, they couldn't believe their eyes.

Their snake was *sticking out of the vent pipe on the roof*, just above the bathroom. It had taken a wrong turn in the pipe and gone *up* instead of down through the main line!

Whipping around on the roof, it had torn off a patch of the old shingles.

"Thanks a lot, boys!" one of the roofers laughed. "You've been doing our job for us!"

The Late Mr. Murch

Everybody is late to work occasionally. Sometimes there's nothing you can do about it – traffic, car problems, family. Happens every once in a while.

But some people are late *all* the time. You know the kind of guy I mean. He rolls in just a little bit late, nearly every day.

That was Harry Murch, who was an electrician at one of the major auto companies in Detroit. You could say one thing for him: he was consistent. He always showed up ten or fifteen minutes into the shift.

And he always had an excuse. Not a *good* excuse, like a sick kid or a death in the family. But his excuses were usually creative – and pretty entertaining.

In fact, a lot of the guys would gather around to hear the latest.

Like when Harry came racing in from the parking lot and said, "Didn't you boys feel the earthquake?"

Earthquake? In Michigan?

"I swear it was an earthquake!" he said, totally serious. "It rattled the whole house in the middle of the night and must've shook my alarm clock off the nightstand! The clock landed on the shut-off button!"

Well, that was one nobody had heard before.

But after a while, Harry got later and later. And his excuses got more and more lame. Once he said that he couldn't leave the house because the cat was asleep in the driveway – and he didn't want to disturb her!

Finally, the foreman had had enough. He was determined to have it out with Harry as he came wandering in late again on day.

"Hey, Murch!" he said. "You're late!"

Harry started to launch into one of his excuses. "I am? Well, what happened is –"

But the foreman cut him off. "I don't wanna hear it! That's fourteen times you've been late this past month! And let me tell you, I'm getting pretty sick of it!"

At this point, the other guys started to gather around to see how Harry was going to handle this. It was almost like watching two kids squaring off for a fight in the schoolyard.

"Fourteen, huh?" Harry said, as if surprised. "I haven't been keeping track."

"You sure haven't!" the foreman yelled at Harry. He was getting more and more ticked off. *"Do you even know what time we start around here?"*

He smiled at the foreman. "I don't have a clue," he said calmly. "You're always working when I get here!"

Everybody broke out laughing. Even the foreman. But that was the last time Harry was late.

Lying Down on the Job

I think everyone will agree that waitresses are the backbone of the workingman's – and workingwoman's – world. After you've put in long, hard hours and you can't get home for a meal, you head for your favorite restaurant or diner. There, it's your regular waitress who usually takes care of you.

And those waitresses have a tough job, too. We often don't appreciate the conditions they have to work under. My friend Joan is a waitress at a small restaurant that does a huge business. The place is almost like a diner, with booths along the wall and a few tables in the middle for larger parties.

In the evening, the place is really hopping. Guys come in from the auto plant across the street, and office workers stop in from the various buildings around the restaurant.

Joan takes care of everybody, without ever seeming to get rattled or flustered. She's a real pro.

But one night, everything just got crazy. Both of the waitresses who worked the counter called in sick, and Joan had to do it all.

Customers were calling out to her from all over the place:

"Hey, Joan, could we have some water over here?"

"What about my bread?"

"Where's my side of potatoes?"

"I ordered the soup, not the salad!"

"This steak is medium, and I wanted it medium well!"

Joan literally ran from one table to the other, stopping by the counter to try to handle everything. And she did it with her usual good humor ... but as the evening went on, even she was starting to fray around the edges.

She was falling farther and farther behind, when a large party sat down at the biggest table and all started ordering the house specialty: lobster.

Since the lobsters are served with the claws, shells, and all, it's a pretty demanding job just to haul all that food out to the table. But Joan did her best, carrying huge platters at a time.

Then one of the people at the table who hadn't been served yet started to get impatient.

"Waitress!" he called out. "Everybody else is almost done, and I haven't even got my food yet!"

"Coming right out, sir!" Joan called from the back of the restaurant. And she hurried through the main aisle, carrying the lobster dinners.

Just at that moment, a woman in a booth started to get up – and put her leg out into the aisle.

You guessed it. As Joan sped by, she tripped over the woman's leg.

Joan staggered forward, trying to regain her balance, but it was no use. She hit the edge of the big table ... lost her footing ... and landed on her butt!

Lobsters went flying everywhere. On top of her, on top of the customers. The restaurant was still as everybody stared in amazement.

Finally one guy at the table brushed some sauce off his shirt and said: "I think we're supposed to *eat* the food, not *wear* it."

Joan broke up laughing ... followed by everyone else. After that performance, the rest of the night was a piece of cake.

Monkey Business

A contractor friend of mine named Leo landed a big job renovating the building that housed a pharmaceutical company. Leo put his people on it right away. He didn't want anything to screw up the smooth completion of the work. It meant a lot of money.

So he was a little worried when the company president called him in to his office.

"Leo," the man said, "something is missing from our laboratory and I suspect one of your men took it."

Leo was shocked. "Whatever it is, I'll make sure the guy returns it – then I'll fire him! What's missing?"

"It's a very valuable *spider monkey* that we were right in the middle of testing with a new drug," the man said. "If we don't get this monkey back, I'm going to look for a new contractor!"

"Don't worry," said Leo. "I'll check into it."

He went around to all the men asking whether they knew about anything missing from the laboratory. He didn't say what it was. Of course, no one admitted a thing. This investigation was going nowhere.

The company president was not happy with the lack of results.

But then Leo had an idea. "I think I can wrap this up," he told the man, "but I'll need your help."

The company president promised to do whatever he could. He just wanted the monkey back.

The next day, all around the job site, new signs appeared. They said DANGER! ESCAPED LAB MONKEY. HIGHLY CONTAGIOUS.

Leo watched carefully as the men read the signs. Most of them just shrugged, but one, a carpenter named Kronk, suddenly seemed very upset.

He ran to Leo. "Boss, I gotta go home early."

"What's wrong, Kronk?" Leo said.

"Uh ... not feeling well. I'm sick. Be back tomorrow."

So Leo let him go. At the end of the day, the site shut down as usual, everyone went home and the parking lot emptied. Except for one car that slipped back in.

A shadowy figure carrying a box hurried from the parking lot to the part of the building that housed the laboratory. Then a few minutes later, the figure returned to the car and took off.

In the morning, Leo called Kronk over. He showed him stills from a video surveillance camera of Kronk sneaking the monkey back into its cage.

Faced with the evidence, Kronk broke down and nervously admitted taking the monkey. "I just *borrowed* him, to bring home and play with my kids!" he said. "Now they're gonna get some terrible disease!"

"Relax," Leo said. "Your kids are okay. There's nothing wrong with the monkey."

"What?!" said Kronk, suddenly angry. "You tricked me!"

"That's right – really made a monkey outta *you*!"

An Ol' Cowhand

This story came to me from out in the West – western Canada. People don't usually think of cowboys as blue-collar, but they certainly are. They're the backbone of the cattle industry, in any country.

Real cowboys work hard and generally have a hard life. So it's not surprising that they need to blow off a little steam now and then. That's what the Calgary Stampede is all about.

It's a rodeo and a chance for the cowboys to compete in various events. They can show off their skills for the crowd, and try to get the best of each other.

Besides the serious events, like calf roping and branding that show real work skills, there are also pure entertainment competitions.

One such is the event where each cowboy tries to see who can throw a saddle on a horse the fastest and then ride to the end of the corral without getting thrown off. Since there was no bridle, they had to just hang onto a rope around the horse's neck.

The horses that are used are not the well-trained cowponies, but ones that are barely broken. They're not yet used to being ridden – and certainly don't like it very much.

This is a very popular event, with lots of crowd participation in cheering for their favorites. And this particular day, the crowd was big and rowdy.

Wayne, Billy, and Pete were among the finalists. They were each ready to take their last ride past the roaring crowd, and man, were they pumped up.

"Gotta stay cool," said Wayne to the other two.

"Yeah," agreed Pete. "Don't let all the noise distract you."

Billy was the youngest. It was his first Stampede, and he was pretty cocky. "I just tune 'em out," he said. "Concentration, that's the key."

Well, it definitely got hard to concentrate as the competition went on. Wayne and Pete racked up good scores, and the crowd went wild.

Then it was Billy's turn. And he really gave them a show.

Besides being fast, he was flashy. He got the saddle on the horse in record time, swung up into it, and grabbed the rope.

"Go for it, kid!" yelled Wayne from the sidelines.

"Watch and learn!" Billy yelled back, grinning.

Then Billy took off for the other side, past the stands and the screaming crowd. He went by them as close as he could, giving them all a good look.

The horse was bucking like crazy, but Billy was hanging on.

Until he got a little too carried away by the crowd. They were cheering and waving so much, that Billy couldn't resist waving back. *With both hands!*

He let go of the rope – and was tossed, ass over teakettle, into the dirt!

As he lay there dazed, Pete came over to help him up. "I watched and learned, all right," he said, laughing.

"Yeah," Billy groaned as he got to his feet. "Concentrate."

Tie One On

This story shows how having a "liquid lunch" can sometimes create problems on the job. It can be downright dangerous in terms of job safety, but it can also provide some funny moments.

Vern, a sheet metal fabricator, told me about the time that he was working high up in the rafters of an auto plant.

He had to carry pieces of sheet metal up stairs, then climb scaffolding to install the material under the roof. Sometimes it took more than a half hour to make his way from the plant floor to the roof.

Well, after a morning of doing this over and over, Vern went out to lunch and had a couple of beers. He thought he'd fortify himself. He wasn't looking forward to an afternoon of hiking up the scaffolding over and over again.

When he got back, Harvey, the foreman, was waiting for him.

"Where've you been?" Harvey asked. "We got a work schedule here!"

"Aw right, aw right," complained Vern. "I'm going back up. Just gimme a minute to get my tools together."

"Look, I've been watching you all morning," said Harvey. "You've been grabbing a piece of material, carrying it up, then coming back down for another one. Let's make it simple."

Harvey brought over a big coil of rope and handed it to Vern.

"What's this for?" Vern asked. He was a little fuzzy from the beers, but was determined not to show it.

Harvey looked at him like he was an idiot. "Here's what you do – climb back up there with the rope, then throw down one end. I'll get an apprentice to tie on a piece of material. Then you just haul it up each time."

"Hey, great idea," said Vern. "I won't have to keep climbing up there!"

"Now you got it," said Harvey, handing him the coil of rope.

As Vern started the long climb up to the roof, Harvey just shook his head. That guy just isn't too smart, he thought to himself.

Vern went up the stairs ... up the scaffolding ... hauled himself up into the high rafters ... and finally reached the spot where he was working, high above the floor.

Now, after the big lunch and the beer, all he wanted to do was take a nap. Looking down at the tiny figure of Harvey, he felt his eyes close. He forced himself to keep them open.

He heard Harvey yell something from down below, but he hadn't been paying attention.

"What?" Vern shouted back. "I didn't hear you!"

"I said," Harvey yelled up, "throw down the rope!"

Vern suddenly remembered what he was supposed to be doing. "Oh yeah," he yelled back. "Here it comes!"

And he pitched the coil of rope down. The *whole* rope.

He forgot to tie one end.

As the rope landed in a pile at his feet, Harvey shook his head again in disgust. "Okay, Vern," he yelled up. "Now you can come back down and start all over again!"

Up in the rafters, Vern groaned. No more "liquid lunches" for him.

Heavy Duty

This one happened to me early in my handyman career. At that time I was taking on any and all jobs that came along. I can truthfully say that most of them were learning experiences.

Especially the first water heater I ever installed.

Actually, it was more of a moving job. A buddy of mine, Rob, and I were hired by the owner of a pet shop to move a big 40-gallon commercial water heater from the old pet shop to the new location down the street.

"Are you boys sure you know what you're doing?" the owner, Mrs. Finch, asked us.

"Oh, no problem," I said confidently. You always had to sound confident no matter what the job was.

"Piece of cake," said Rob, acting just as sure of himself.

Mrs. Finch nodded. I don't know whether she believed us or not, but she left us to it. As soon as she'd gone, we both looked at each other.

"Okay, so now what?" asked Rob.

I shrugged. "We take it apart, haul it down the street, and re-install it. How hard can that be?"

"Not too hard," he said. "Let's do it!"

We turned off the water and disconnected the pipes without too much trouble. The water heater wasn't very old, and the joints weren't rusted. So far so good.

"Hey, no sweat!" said Rob, pleased with our progress so far.

Next step was to move the water heater tank itself. We both grabbed hold of it and shifted it out of its old position. We could hardly budge it, the thing was so heavy!

But we struggled and struggled, kind of half-sliding and half-walking the tank to the door of the pet shop. Thank goodness we didn't have to go up any stairs or we wouldn't have made it.

Just outside we had a small hand truck or dolly that we were able to slide under the tank, tip it back, and roll it the rest of the way out of the pet shop.

Even with the dolly, it was a tough job. We stood the tank up in the pickup bed – after denting the side and scraping it up a bit. But what could we do? It was so heavy and bulky we could hardly control it.

Anyway, we drove it down to the new pet shop location, got it off the truck and inside, and hooked it up again. With the dents and scrapes, it didn't look too good ... but it worked just fine. We were pretty proud of ourselves.

Then Mrs. Finch came by to check on our progress. She took one look at the water heater and was horrified. "What did you boys do, drag it behind your truck?!" she exclaimed.

We tried to explain that it was really, really heavy and hard to move and –

She cut us off. "Did you ever think of *draining the water out of it first?!*" she demanded.

Guess we should have thought of that. Well, I said it was a learning experience.

Cracked

You know the old saying that every appliance repairman or plumber has to show his butt-crack while working. Everybody's seen it happen: the guy squats down on his haunches with his back turned, and ... there it is in all its glory! It also seems like the older a guy is, the more crack he shows.

Anyway, that's what was happening all day long when a plumber named Stan was laying drainage pipe with his crew. He was a middle-aged guy who did everything the old-fashioned way. But the younger guys who worked with him didn't care for one tradition – the ol' bare butt-crack, always visible above the belt line.

So Brian, the prankster of the crew, decided he'd had enough. He crept down into the ditch where Stan was working, bent over as usual. Motioning to the other men to be quiet, Brian sneaked up behind Stan and picked up a dry handful of fine, silt-like sand.

Then he poured it down the back of Stan's pants!

Stan came bellowing up out of the ditch like a wounded bear and went after Brian, roaring with fury. The foreman had to separate them as all the men howled with laughter.

When the foreman asked why Brian had done it, he just shrugged. "Aw, we were just tired of lookin' at Stan's butt-crack all day," he said.

The Runaway

My friend Gene was a car mechanic and worked long hours. His one escape was taking the family to their favorite campsite in northern Michigan, on one of the larger lakes. They liked to do everything on that lake – swim, fish, cook out on the beach, or just cruise around in their boat.

And when Gene got a new Mariner outboard for the boat, it was a big day. With the new motor, they could roam farther around the lake and stay out longer on the water.

So Gene loaded the kids and his wife into the boat and headed off into the middle of the lake. He noticed a strange vibration, and it wasn't from the waves. What could it be? The motor had been tested, checked out from top to bottom, so it couldn't be that ... could it?

Suddenly, the outboard gave a lurch – and jumped right off the back of the boat! Propeller spinning, it almost seemed to take off by itself, just before it plunged to the bottom of the lake!

Gene and the family were stunned. What had happened? When Gene looked closer, he saw the problem. He had forgotten to tighten the tie-down brackets on the motor.

And Gene wasn't a happy camper when he had to paddle back by hand – and then hire a diver in town to go after the new outboard.

Play ... and Pay

This is a story that sounds like it was made up. And that's what I'd think, too, if I didn't know the guys it happened to. They swear it's true – and they have the empty bank accounts to prove it! Here's what they told me ...

My buddy Phil and three of his friends were moose-hunting in northern Canada. They had been hiking through the woods for most of the day, and they were tired.

The tracks they were following finally led them across a rough trail ... and right into fenced-off farmland. They couldn't go any farther without crossing private land. Besides that, it looked like a big farm. To go around would take the rest of the day, and then they might lose the tracks. What to do?

"I say we just duck under the fence and go across," said one of the guys."

Phil pointed to the nearby farmhouse. "The farmer'll see us," he said. "Let's just go over and ask permission. What can it hurt?"

"I dunno," said one of the others. "People around here don't care much for hunters."

But the other guys gave in and followed Phil to the farmhouse. They waited in the yard while Phil went up to the door. Some scrawny looking cows were standing around by the run-down barn. In fact, the whole place looked pretty shabby.

Phil knocked at the door, and the farmer opened it. The old man scowled at him as Phil politely asked if they could cross his land. To Phil's surprise, the farmer agreed right away.

"Before you go," he said, "I wonder if you could do me a favor."

"Sure," said Phil. "Be glad to."

"My horse is lying out there in the barn. He's old and sick, and I'd like to put him out of his misery. But I can't bring myself to do it. Do you suppose you could shoot him for me?"

"No problem," said Phil.

The farmer closed the door, and Phil started back down the steps.

Suddenly he got an idea for a gag on his buddies. I'll just have a little fun with them, he thought. He put on an angry look and pretended he was really ticked off.

Phil stomped off toward the barn, unslinging his rifle.

"Hey!" one of the guys yelled to him. "What'd the old man say?"

"Won't let us cross his land!" Phil yelled back. "I'll show him!"

Phil went into the barn and found the old horse, who was almost gone anyway. A quick shot finished him.

He heard one of the others yell from outside, "What the hell did you do?"

"Shot his horse!" Phil shouted back. "That'll teach him!"

Phil made a final check on the horse and was about to leave the barn, when he heard three shots from outside.

What's going on? he wondered, and ran out of the barn.

There were his buddies, lowering their rifles. Lying dead in the yard were the farmer's three cows!

"Guess we showed him, too!" said one of his buddies.

Phil couldn't believe it. And here came the old farmer out of his house, yelling about calling the police!

Well, as it turned out, he didn't call the police. Phil and the boys straightened everything out ... to the tune of $2100 for the moth-eaten old cattle!

Next year they vowed to *walk around* any farm they came to.

Pump It Up

Working heavy commercial/industrial plumbing jobs like I do is tough enough, but doing it in the dead of winter? That's something else. Your tools get a coating of ice on them, and sometimes they freeze right to your hand!

But not everybody understands how the cold weather slows down a job. Sometimes not even the people in charge of it do.

I was installing fire mains at a plywood mill in northern Ontario one winter. I don't even know how cold it was, but you can just imagine.

The mill itself was up on a hill. Down below was a pond, which was where we had installed twelve-inch piping below the ground, to tap into the pond water for the fire mains. Just beyond the edge of the pond, the pipe took a ninety-degree turn at an underground elbow and went up vertically. Above ground, it then ran on up to the mill.

So that's the scene. But it takes one more thing to complete it: Duane, the company's rep, who was in charge of making sure the job went smoothly. I don't know where they got this guy, but he didn't know squat about the work.

Now picture this: Duane set himself up nice and cozy on the frozen surface of the pond. He had a lawn chair, a radio, a newspaper, a hot drink ... and a comfy snowmobile suit. Not only that, but he had built himself a roaring fire, right on the ice!

From this cozy spot, he could watch the rest of us freeze our butts off laying pipe. From time to time he'd yell out orders. We weren't too happy about it ... but we had to put up with him.

Then the day finally came when we had to pressure-test the connections.

Duane was in his usual spot, supervising the proceedings from his lawn chair on the ice. "All right – turn on the pumps!" he yelled.

It was all going pretty smoothly. We monitored the pressure as it gradually built up, pumping water out of the pond. No problems so far.

Duane wasn't really paying much attention. He was stoking his bonfire and sipping hot coffee.

But he was also looking nervously at his watch. The test had to be finished in the next fifteen minutes. He had promised his boss at the mill. But it was going too slowly.

"More pressure!" Duane yelled to the guy controlling the pumps. "Let's speed it up!"

The pump man knew that wasn't a good idea and tried to tell Duane. But it was no use. Duane wouldn't listen.

"I've never made a mistake in this company, and I'm not going to start now! More pressure! Really goose it!" he yelled.

The pump man goosed it.

And the elbow in the ground blew. The water shot straight up out of the broken pipe like Old Faithful! Only a *lot* colder. It poured down on Duane, scattering his cozy fire, lawn chair, newspaper, radio, and hot coffee. And soaking his comfy snowmobile suit.

Guess Duane just made his first mistake.

We would've laughed a lot harder, but we knew we were just going to have to put it all back together again!

"Fur" Cryin' Out Loud!

My friend Susie works for a contractor doing home renovations. Of course, she uses a drill a lot in her line of work. It's a necessary tool, and sometimes it gets her in trouble. But this time, it wasn't her, exactly, even though she was ultimately responsible.

Here's what she told me happened ...

She often has a helper, to carry tools, run wires with her, clean up, or just plain speed things along. This one day, Justin was with her.

He was a good guy, but sometimes not too bright. Although he could do any job she gave him. However, she did have to supervise him pretty closely so he'd stay focused and not get off track. Justin also had a tendency to jump to conclusions.

So they were at the end of a long day – a long three days, actually, working at the house of a wealthy older couple. Susie was dead tired, too, and was sure going to be glad when it was all over. One of their last jobs was to install a handrail in the tub of a very fancy bathroom.

Susie measured everything, marked it, and gave Justin the job of drilling holes in the tile wall. It was a simple job, but she was just too beat to watch him carefully. So she busied herself doing some clean-up.

Justin started drilling into the wall, and everything was going fine ... until she heard him yell for her.

"Come here, quick!" he shouted. "Look at this!"

She rushed over, still really tired. Justin held out the drill bit he had just pulled from the wall. Wrapped around the end was a big fuzzy ball of ... *fur.*

Susie wasn't sure what she was looking at. She reached out and felt it. It was some kind of fur, all right.

"There's a dead animal trapped in the wall!" Justin said. He looked at her, wide-eyed. "Maybe we should finish up like nothing was wrong and keep our mouths shut."

She shook her head. "We can't do that." She felt the ball of fur again. It was very soft and thick. "If this is some kinda animal, sooner or later it's going to stink up the whole house. It's gotta come outta there. We have to tell Carlos." Carlos was the homeowner.

"Tell me what?" Carlos said, walking in.

So Susie took a deep breath and told him.

"Are you sure?" he asked.

She was really tired and not thinking too clearly … so she said yes, she was pretty sure there was a dead animal in the wall.

That was all Carlos needed. He told them to rip open the wall.

That's what they did. Pieces of fancy tile lay broken and scattered over the floor.

But there was no animal in there.

They looked at each other. They looked at the ball of fur on the end of the drill bit. Then they saw what was on the *other* side of the bathroom wall, the next room that Justin had drilled into.

Carlos's wife's closet.

With a sinking feeling, Susie stuck her finger in through the hole and felt fur. It was the sleeve of his wife's *mink coat*. The drill had gone right through and ripped a chunk out of the *very* expensive fur!

Carlos was not happy. And, as you might expect, the contractor was not too happy about the report that Susie had to make.

Fly-Wood

Alan was on a clean-up crew at the construction site of a big office building in Chicago. The job was almost finished, and there was a lot of debris still left to be loaded on the trucks.

The crew worked steadily ... but they were slowed down a bit because of wind. You know Chicago's nickname – the windy city. And it sure was. Some pretty heavy pieces of building material got moved around to an amazing degree. Sometimes the guys had to chase down chunks of drywall, rolls of insulation, even metal ductwork.

That's why Alan's foreman was a little nervous about the stack of 4x8 plywood that was starting to flutter in the wind like a giant deck of cards.

The foreman told Alan and several other guys to move the plywood into the trucks next, and be quick about it. Alan grabbed one, started to pick it up, and the wind tugged at it. "I got it!" he yelled – just as the wind yanked it out of his hands. "No, I don't!" he shouted.

The big sheet of plywood spun through the air like a frisbee – and crashed through a window all the way up on the second floor!

Delivered as Promised

Now I want to tell you about something that happened to me and my friend Jimmy when we were hauling a load of logs in Canada, up in northern Ontario. These were pine logs, all about thirty feet in length. Big suckers.

The two of us were in the truck's cab, a Mack Elite, with the flatbed trailer hitched to the back. After loading with the truck's picker, I made sure the chains were tight over the logs and they weren't going anywhere.

I know what you're thinking: "He's going to tell us how the logs broke loose and rolled all over the road. Big Deal." Well, that's not exactly what happened ....

Jimmy and I were just watching the scenery roll by, talking about nothing in particular. He was driving as we came up over a hill and started down a pretty steep incline. Down at the bottom of the hill was our destination, the sawmill where we would be offloading the logs. As I spotted it, I suddenly remembered something.

I turned to Jimmy. "You sent Orville the sample, didn't you?" Orville was the sawmill manager.

"What sample?" he asked.

"The timber sample we were supposed to send him."

"Oh, *that* sample. I thought you sent it."

"I thought *you* did," I said, getting a little ticked off.

"Not me."

"That's just great! He wanted to see what he was getting *before* we brought the whole load!"

Suddenly there was a strange *ka-chunk* sound from the rear, and the truck lurched. Jimmy immediately eased on the brakes. I caught sight of something in the side mirror, moving up on us. Was another truck trying to pass?

I thought to myself, No, it can't be! But then we both turned to look out my side window ... and we couldn't believe what we were seeing.

The trailer, fully loaded with logs, *was passing us on the right!*

It had broken loose from the hitch and was heading down the hill ahead of us – directly at the sawmill!

"Y'know," Jimmy said, strangely calm, "I think Orville's gonna get to see those logs before he sees us, after all."

The trailer continued on down the hill, gaining speed all the way. We could see tiny figures all around the sawmill running in every direction.

Fortunately, the trailer veered off the road at the last second and dumped the entire load over an embankment – right in front of the sawmill! The spilled logs looked like giant matchsticks, scattered everywhere.

One log actually rolled up to the sawmill door, just as Orville stepped out. He sure got his sample!

And Jimmy and I spent quite a few hours with the picker, dragging those logs back over the embankment.

Wake-Up Call

There are a lot of dangerous jobs in a steel mill. Everyone knows that working around the furnaces or anywhere there is molten metal is risky. But you don't often think of pipefitters at a steel mill as having a particularly hazardous job.

Well, the guys who told me this story sure did. They were working on a "highline," which is a kind of pipe bridge over this fast-moving river by the mill. The whole structure arched about 190 feet above the water.

Just imagine working that high up, with all your tools and material, trying to do the job and keep from falling off!

Two of the men who knew how tough it was were Sam and Carl, who had to go up on the highline day after day. During a particularly windy day, they decided they'd had enough. They called the foreman over.

"We're not going up there again until you figure out some kind of safety net!" Sam said.

"Safety net?" the foreman asked. "What're you talkin' about?"

Carl piped in: "We could fall off the highline, into the river and get swept away downstream before you know it!"

"Okay," the foreman agreed. "I can't string a net across the river but I got an idea ..."

He called over one of the laborers, Fat Eddie, and gave him a new job. Fat Eddie was to get into a small boat with an outboard and anchor in the middle of the river, under the highline. Then, if one of the workers fell into the river, Fat Eddie could pick them up.

Sam and Carl didn't much like the idea, since Fat Eddie wasn't exactly the sharpest guy to trust with your life ... but what could they do? They went back up on the high pipes.

Everything went smoothly. In fact, it was beginning to look like Fat Eddie had the sack job! While Sam and Carl busted their butts working on the pipes, they could look down on Fat Eddie, just floating around in his boat.

Some days, he'd read the paper, some days he'd munch doughnuts and listen to his radio, and some days he'd even watch the little battery-powered TV he brought. It was like a floating one-man party! The rest of the guys were getting pretty ticked off.

Then one day they looked down to see Fat Eddie taking a nap in the sun. He was perfectly contented.

"Look at him down there!" Carl said angrily. "I can't stand it. We gotta do something."

Sam grinned slyly. "Hand me that length of pipe, and I'll show you a little trick," he said.

Sam got out his level and made Carl hold the other end of the pipe while he steadied it. When it was perfectly level, he signaled to Carl. "Let go!" he said.

The length of pipe dropped exactly flat to the surface of the water and hit right near Fat Eddie's boat – with a sound like a cannon shot!

Fat Eddie leaped up, and was so startled that he had, well, an "accident." How can I put this? Let's just say a quick change of pants suddenly became necessary.

Then Sam and Carl nearly *did* fall off the highline from laughing.

A Real Housecleaning

I recently heard about a house-cleaning service that had a communication problem. I mean, a *real* communication problem. This was in one of the wealthier areas of Los Angeles, and the service specialized in preparing houses for parties.

As you might expect, there's a good business for that in L.A. At least there would be for this company – if it could ever get its act together.

We'll call it Acme Housecleaning. A lot of people in L.A. are famous for something, and Acme was famous for not calling back and not showing up on time.

You'd think they would be out of business pretty quick with a reputation like that. But that wasn't the case. People still kept calling and giving them another chance.

I know of one homeowner, though, who finally had enough. The Ripleys called Acme before a big party they had scheduled.

The day before the party ... no Acme. The Ripleys were getting worried. The *morning* of the party – still no Acme. Now they were getting mad, and they were forced to rush around themselves, cleaning the place up. Acme never did show up.

But the president of the company called Mr. Ripley and apologized. He said that one of their trucks didn't get its dispatch messages, and he begged for another chance.

Well, it so happened that the Ripleys were having another party coming up, so Mr. Ripley agreed to try them one more time.

"But make sure you tell your cleaning person not to turn on the water in the upstairs tub," Mr. Ripley told the Acme president. "We're having some trouble with it."

"No problem," said the Acme guy. "I'll make sure Connie gets the word."

This time, the day before the party, Connie arrived from Acme. The Ripleys were leaving to do last-minute shopping all day, so they let her in and told her to start cleaning upstairs. Then they rushed out.

Naturally Connie started in the upstairs bathroom. And turned on the faucet in the tub ... which stuck open, going full blast! Connie was rattled and flipped the drain lever – but it stuck *closed!*

Now the tub was rapidly filling.

In a panic, Connie remembered that she had a pair of pliers in her van that she could use to turn off the faucet. She ran downstairs and out the door ... which slammed shut behind her.

She was locked out.

Connie grabbed her cell phone in the van and frantically called the company.

"Oh, Connie," said the Acme dispatcher. "Glad you called. I have a message for you – don't turn on the tub faucet in the Ripleys' upstairs bathroom."

"Now you tell me!" Connie shrieked, as she looked through the window and saw water pouring down the stairs!

Well, it was two hours before the Ripleys could be contacted. The living room ceiling fell in, the party was canceled ... and they never called Acme again.

I Smell Trouble

I heard this story from a security guard in a downtown Detroit office building. Believe me, these guys have some tales to tell. They see anything and everything, especially on the night shift.

Anyway, Sal told me about one night when he and his partner Jerry were making their rounds of the building just about closing time. People were leaving, they were locking the doors, and getting ready for a quiet night.

Sal was about ready to turn out the lights in one long hallway when Jerry stopped him.

"Hold it. What's that?" he said, pointing.

Sal looked down the hallway and thought he saw the running figure of a man.

"I think we got an intruder," Sal said. "Let's go!"

They took off down the hall, but at the end there was no one. Just another empty hallway around the corner.

Sal grabbed his walkie-talkie. "All stations," he said into it. "Possible intruder sighted on level two, north hall."

But almost before Sal could finish, other parts of the building were calling in. Other guards had spotted someone, too. Now they knew something was up. And they couldn't take any chances.

Everybody was starting to get a little nervous because they didn't know what they had. Who was running through the building and what was he doing?

The guards in the other areas of the building started systematically going through the hallways, hoping to flush out whoever was in there.

It wasn't long before Sal and Jerry saw the figure running toward them!

"Hold it!" Sal yelled.

But the man kept coming.

Sal and Jerry didn't want to do it, but they pulled their guns and aimed.

"Stop right there," Jerry yelled.

The man tried to turn the corner and duck down another hallway – but two other security guards boxed him in. He was backed up against a wall as the four guards came toward him. Sal shined his flashlight beam at him.

Suddenly the man started to fumble in one of his pockets. Sal saw a suspicious-looking bulge.

The man jerked something from the pocket ... and in the flashlight beam it gleamed like metal.

All the guards aimed their weapons.

"Drop it!" Sal bellowed. *"Now!"*

Startled, the man tossed the shiny object to the floor. It hit with a *splat!*

What the hell?

Lying there on the floor in front of them was ... a *fish!*

The guards advanced on the frightened man, their guns still drawn.

"Hey, I know this guy," Jerry said. "It's old Burt! He hangs around outside bumming spare change from people. He's a little nuts. I think he was just looking for a warm place to sleep."

"Th ... that's right," said Burt nervously. "Please let me keep my lucky fish! I carry one everywhere."

"Lucky fish?" laughed Sal, as the guards all put their guns away. "Well, it sure worked for you, pal. You're lucky we didn't shoot you!"

Bailing Out

Ben and Matt, a couple of pipefitters I know, told me this story about rushing to make an important union meeting. They were both late getting off work, and the meeting was that night. After grabbing a quick bite to eat, they hurried to Matt's house to take showers.

Matt had a big green parrot as a pet. It didn't really talk much, but it could do tricks. It loved to grab at anything that dangled down in front of it – a ball on a string, a banana ... anything. It also got very excited when it heard water running. It would fly around and make for the running water, shrieking its head off.

Well, the two guys were in such a hurry, Matt forgot to tell Ben about the parrot. Ben climbed into the shower stall, which was open on two sides, with a curtain over each.

When Ben turned the water on, the parrot went crazy and dove for the shower. All Matt could think of was how the parrot tried to bite anything that dangled ... Oh oh.

"Ben – get outta the shower! Fast!" Matt yelled.

Not knowing *what* the heck was going on, Ben leaped out one side of the stall, with the curtain wrapped around him – while the parrot flew in the other!

Safe!

Slow Boat Afloat

Here's a story a friend told me about his parents, Jack and Helen, who ran a boat rental business for many years on one of the lakes in northern Michigan. They rented boats for fishing, water skiing, or just plain pleasure cruising.

Jack didn't quite know what to make of a young woman who stopped by and rented a 26-foot Sea Ray with a big Evinrude outboard on the back. He could tell that she didn't exactly seem to know what she was doing.

For one thing, her cell phone rang constantly while Helen was explaining how the outboard worked. She wasn't really paying attention to any of the instructions Helen gave her. She kept telling Helen, "Sure, sure, I know all that. How hard can it be?" ... in between phone calls.

As she drove away with the boat trailer hitched to her big SUV, Jack turned to Helen. "We'll be hearing from her again before the day's over."

Sure enough, Jack's phone rang a couple of hours later. It was the woman calling.

"What's the problem?" Jack asked.

"Well," she said, "I like the boat fine, I've been all around the lake on it, but it's just too slow. I think something's wrong."

Jack mentioned a few items to check on the outboard. She said she'd try those and call back.

"Do you think she can fix it?" Helen asked him after he hung up.

"I don't hold out any great hopes," Jack said, shaking his head.

It wasn't long before the woman did call back with the same complaint: "I checked everything you said, and the boat's still just *too slow,*" she said. "I think I need a bigger motor!"

"That Evinrude that's on there is plenty big enough," Jack said. "I can't imagine what's wrong."

"Maybe you'd better come out here and take a look at it," the woman said. "Please hurry!"

"Be right there," said Jack with a sigh. That was the last thing he wanted to do. But ... you had to take care of the customers.

When he arrived at the dock, there was the woman, frantically waving her arms. In the water next to her was the Sea Ray. Jack couldn't see anything wrong, except maybe the boat was riding a little low in the water.

"Thank goodness you're here!" the woman cried. "I have people coming to ski in less than an hour. *Do something!*"

"I'll try," Jack said, looking around the boat launch. "Say ... where's the trailer?"

The woman looked blank. "What trailer?"

"The trailer you brought the boat here with."

"I haven't seen it," said the woman, looking puzzled.

Just then Jack happened to glance down into the water by the boat. He caught a glimpse under the water of chrome, metal, rubber tires ....

It couldn't be, he thought. But it was.

The trailer was still attached to the boat!

She had been driving around the lake with the trailer hanging underneath it!

Lost & Found

Awhile back, Roxy, a plumber friend of mine, got a call from a long-time customer of hers, an older gentleman named Walter. For an experienced professional like her, it seemed like a pretty routine job. He was having trouble with a blocked-up toilet.

So she packed up her toilet auger and went over to his house to take a look. She figured she would be there a little longer than usual because Walter liked to talk. He'd been in the military all his life and had plenty of stories that he liked to tell now that he was retired.

Roxy actually thought a lot of it was pretty interesting, and figured she could listen while she worked. That was what usually happened. But this time it was different.

When Walter greeted her at the door and let her in, he was totally silent. He smiled and showed her to the bathroom where the problem toilet was … but he didn't say a word. That wasn't like him. He had a strange look on his face, too. She wondered what was going on.

Roxy tried to start a conversation, but Walter just smiled again and shrugged. Oh well, she thought, maybe he just doesn't feel like gabbing today. That was fine with her. Maybe she'd get the job done and get out of there a little sooner.

She brought in her tools and got ready to check out the toilet, which was stopped up, all right. Meanwhile, Walter busied himself around the house.

He seemed to be looking for something, turning over cushions of the couch, opening drawers, peering under furniture. He was shaking his head, a little upset that he couldn't find whatever he was searching for.

"Hey, Walter," Roxy said, "what's going on?"

But still not a word.

So she went to work on the toilet, feeding the auger down … until it hit whatever the obstruction was. It was something hard.

As she wiggled the auger around, trying to snag the blockage that was down there, Walter gave up on whatever he was looking for and came into the bathroom to watch.

"Lose something?" Roxy asked.

Sadly, he just nodded.

"Well, it'll turn up," she said.

Suddenly she felt something catch on the end of the auger. Bingo! she slowly rewound it, pulling out of the pipe whatever was blocking it.

And there in the bottom of the toilet bowl was ... a pair of *false teeth!*

She heard a gasp from Walter. Since she didn't particularly want to reach into the toilet water and grab the teeth with her bare hand, she used a large pair of channel-lock pliers to carefully pull them out of the water.

"Oh – there they are!" Walter exclaimed happily. His wide smile showed why he had been close-mouthed all this time: his teeth were missing!

Before Roxy could do anything, he grabbed his teeth from her, turned on the faucet in the nearby sink, and ran them under the water briefly.

Then popped them right into his mouth and grinned!

"Been looking for those for a couple of days!" he said. "Can't talk without my teeth!"

Raccoon in a Basket

One of the side jobs I've had over the years is as a trapper, mostly of nuisance animals in and around the city and suburbs. Every so often a customer will call in a panic for me to get rid of an unwanted visitor.

Well, that's what happened late one afternoon when I was about to go out to dinner with a lady friend. I was all dressed up, even had on my good pair of cowboy boots!

It wasn't a customer calling this time, but it was a painter friend of mine named George who was working with his crew at a beautiful rustic house out in a wooded area. He said that I had to come quick! Emergency! And I had to bring my trapping equipment.

Before I could ask him what the problem was, he hung up.

Now, during my thirty-five years as a plumber and handyman, I've always made it my policy to drop what I'm doing and try to help out the person in trouble. Within reason, of course.

So I cancelled my dinner plans and headed for the address George had given me.

As I pulled into the long driveway, I saw him and his other painters sort of milling around nervously by the entrance to the big garage. George rushed over to my truck.

"Man, are we glad you're here!" he said. "You gotta do something before the customer gets home!"

"Calm down," I said. "What's the problem?"

He led me over to the open garage and pointed inside to the far wall. A bike hung on a rack about halfway up the wall. It had a wire basket attached to the handlebars in front.

And in the basket sat a huge, fat *raccoon* ... staring back at us.

"You've got to get it out of here!" George said. "Quick!"

He told me that the painters were working in the garage and scared the raccoon when it wandered in, so it ran up the wall into the bike basket. They were just as scared and ran out of the garage.

I went back to my truck and got my noose pole, a long tool with a loop on the end that can be slipped around an animal's neck and then tightened to hold it safely and securely.

There was an eight-foot ladder in the garage, and I carefully set it up next to the bike, as the raccoon watched me.

"Somebody hold the ladder," I said, and one of the painters held it as I climbed up toward the raccoon.

An eight-foot ladder is pretty high and a little shaky, especially when you don't know exactly what you're going to do. But as I reached the top few steps, I slipped the noose around the raccoon's neck and tightened it.

He didn't like that at all.

He snarled at me, showed some nasty white teeth, and came flying out of the basket. I still held the pole, with the noose attached to the raccoon – as he swung down like a pendulum!

The painter who was supposed to be holding the ladder let go and ran. I almost fell off ... and everybody else scattered out of the garage!

But I managed to hang onto the pole – and the raccoon – as I led him out, hissing and struggling, to a cage in my truck.

Once he was safely locked up, I looked around. Where was everybody?

They were down at the end of the driveway – as far from that raccoon as they could get!